The Shearer Method

Classic Guitar Developments

By Aaron Shearer, Thomas Kikta and Dr. Alan Hirsh

Editing and Additional Content: **Alan Hirsh, Thomas Kikta**

All Compositions and Arrangements: **Alan Hirsh**

Layout Artist and Cover Design: **James Manly**

Cover Photograph: **Dave Garson**

Camera Operator: **Michael McElligott**

Audio Engineer: **Thomas Kikta**

Video Editor: **Thomas Kikta**

DVD Mastering: **Jamey Stewart - Mega Media Factory**

TNT2 Mastering: **Eric Fortin**

CD Performances: **Thomas Kikta Classic Guitar**

Guitar by: **John Martin Oribe - José Oribe & Co.**

Opening and Closing Voice Over: **Jeff Bergman**

Voice Over Engineer: **Brad Braithwaite**

Physical Therapy Consultant: **Brittany Findley, DPT**

Video and Audio Recorded at: **Brookside Studios, Pittsburgh, PA; Innovative Artists Studios, Santa Monica, CA; Duquesne University Aaron Shearer Memorial Classic Guitar Studio; The Dr. Thomas D. Pappert Center for Performance and Innovation, Pittsburgh, PA**

DVD Manufacturing: **Jesse Naus - Red Caiman Media Studios**

Special Thanks to Dr. Edward Kocher Dean of the Mary Pappert School of Music, Duquesne University, Aaron Stang, Lorraine Shearer, and Patti Kikta.

Dedicated to the memory of Aaron Shearer, Thomas J Kikta, M. Agnes Kikta and Leslie Weidner.

Printed in USA

Aaron Shearer was one of the most widely recognized and respected classic guitar teachers in America. When Shearer started the Classic Guitar Department at American University it became the first classic guitar program in an American institution of higher learning. Subsequently, he was director of the guitar programs at Catholic University of America, Peabody Conservatory of Music, and the North Carolina School of the Arts. Towards the end of his life he was adjunct professor of Classic Guitar at Duquesne University. Mr. Shearer lectured throughout the United States and Canada, and received numerous citations for his contributions to guitar pedagogy. Shearer also became the first classic guitar teacher to be cited for exceptional leadership and merit by the American String Teachers Association and in 1992 received an Honorary Doctorate from Duquesne University.

During his lifetime he published numerous books and articles, including a six-book method entitled *Classic Guitar Technique* which included two volumes with three supplements and a guitar note speller. This benchmark method was originally published in 1959 and is now updated with CD in its 3rd edition by Alfred Publications. In 1992, Mr. Shearer published a three-part book entitled *Learning the Classic Guitar.* Shortly after, he began to experiment with alternative ways of supporting the guitar while still maintaining muscular alignment and full access to the instrument. His creation of the *Shearer Strap* has given guitarists freedom from the constraints of the footstool. In the early part of 2008, prior to his passing, He finished his magnum opus *The Shearer Method,* a comprehensive treatise that covers his entire approach to teaching and learning the classic guitar.

Aaron Shearer's body of work was revolutionary and his unwavering commitment to excellence earned him the moniker, "The Wall," by some of his students. The guitar world has referred to him, as "The Father of the American Classic Guitar". The Guitar Foundation of America has called him "the most prominent pedagogue of the twentieth century". Aaron Shearer's wisdom and insight are sorely missed, but his work and legacy will live on through the Aaron Shearer Foundation and all the lives he has touched.

Thomas Kikta as a musician, producer, professor and author is a versatile artist who has been the director of Classic Guitar and Recording Arts and Sciences at Duquesne University in Pittsburgh, PA. for over twenty five years.

A native of Pittsburgh, he studied Classic Guitar performance with Aaron Shearer at both the Peabody Conservatory and at the North Carolina School of the Arts. He has performed around the country and for such dignitaries as Maya Angelou and Toni Morrison and has worked with such artists as Ricardo Cobo, and Manuel Barrueco. After working closely with Aaron Shearer for over 28 years he with Mr. Shearer co-authored the 3rd edition of the best-selling and benchmark work *Classic Guitar Technique Vol 1* published by Alfred Publications, which was nominated for "Best Instructional Book or Video for 2009" by Music and Sound Retailer. He was invited to write *The Complete Idiots Guide to Classical Guitar Favorites* which was published by Alfred Publications in 2010. This work provides supplementary lessons to 30 favorite selections for a student working with a method book. In 2012 Kikta co-authored *The Shearer Method- Classic Guitar Foundations,* the first in a series of works that defines Shearer's teaching approach.

As a co-founder and Board Chairman of the Guitar Society of Fine Arts, Pittsburgh audiences have enjoyed a decade of world-class guitar music as well as free music lessons for underprivileged children. Thomas Kikta along with members of the Shearer family have founded the Aaron Shearer Foundation, an organization dedicated to preserving and propagating the teachings and legacy of this revolutionary guitar pedagogue.

Dr. Alan Hirsh is a composer, guitarist, and music educator living in North Carolina. He received his Bachelor's in Composition from the University of Arizona and his Masters and Doctorate from the Peabody Conservatory of the Johns Hopkins University. Alan Hirsh is the Music Director and Fine Arts Department Chair at Bishop McGuinness High School in Kernersville, NC. He also teaches guitar at Wake Forest University in Winston-Salem, and is the founder and director of the Piedmont Guitar Orchestra, since 1996. He actively directs clinics and festival guitar orchestras around the country and serves on the executive board of the Aaron Shearer Foundation as well as the Piedmont Classic Guitar Society. Hirsh has composed and arranged extensively for orchestra, band, chorus, guitar and guitar ensemble with works performed around the world. In 1984, he collaborated with Aaron Shearer, composing music for the three-volume method, *Learning the Classic Guitar.* Hirsh's other published guitar works include *Twenty Etudes in fixed Positions, New Music for Classic Guitar, Trio Concertino, Holiday, Folk, Sacred, and Renaissance Collections* for guitar ensemble, music for *The Shearer Method Book Series* as well as an extensive online catalogue of guitar ensemble music.

Table of Contents

Forward

Aaron Shearer first started talking about writing *The Shearer Method* around 1998. He wanted an opportunity to re-define his methodology and share his thoughts and insights from over 70 years of playing and teaching the classic guitar. In the beginning of 2008, towards the end of his life, he came to me with a finished manuscript and said "here it is.... shoot the videos, write the forward and get it published." His original manuscript was quite sizeable in content; thus it became necessary to divide the work into separate publications.

Collaborating with composer Alan Hirsh, our task of bringing the Shearer Method to life was three-fold: 1) visually support, as much as possible, the presentation of technique with easy-to-understand videos; 2) compose a creative new body of music which applies the technique in interesting ways and is available in a controllable audio format to aid the student in practice; and 3) establish an online supplement for some of Shearer's more in-depth extensive writings as well as offerings of added music and video. Collectively this unique approach, truly makes this series stand out as a one-of-a-kind multi-media learning experience.

Book 1: The Shearer Method Classic Guitar Foundations is the first in the series that defines Aaron Shearer's approach to **how** to *begin* the guitar. This work starts the student to read and play while following a logical, unfolding curriculum that supports positive habits for efficient study. The student progresses to a point where playing truly interesting and beautiful music is possible and leaves with a solid technical and musical foundation that prepares them for more challenging horizons.

Book 2: The Shearer Method Classic Guitar Developments picks up where the first book leaves off introducing warm-ups, rest stroke, continuing visualization for memorization, chord development, barring, slurring, rhythmic study and music reading in 12 keys in the open-position. The goal is to acquire the necessary skill set to approach standard repertoire such as that found in *Repertoire From The Masters* presented at the end of the book.

From here the student is prepared to begin to ascend the neck for the purpose of instant recognition of notes along the finger board, the focus of future publications.

We hope that this common-sense approach will serve you well in helping to achieve your goal of not only learning to play the guitar but understanding *how* you play the guitar. It has been an honor to work on this project, to be a part of the talented team that made this a reality and to be a member of the network that carries on Aaron Shearer's legacy. He has truly given us a gift that we all benefit from.... and now you will too.

Enjoy

Thomas Kikta and Alan Hirsh

The Shearer Method
Classic Guitar Developments

Preface

During the years since writing my *Learning the Classic Guitar* Books my approach to guitar study has undergone a number of significant improvements. Although many of the terms and ideas remain the same, some differ in application, others have been replaced, and some important new ones have been added. The current approach (which includes multi-media files for both video and audio) presents a shift in emphasis, both from my previous books, and from other guitar methods I have seen.

This shift in emphasis reflects my conviction about the goal of guitar study: developing the ability to perform well with security and confidence. Performance, for our purposes, means playing for an attentive audience—be it in a concert hall or one's own home. Although the word 'well' may seem self-explanatory, in this text it conveys the special meaning of consistently fulfilling the artistic expectations of both the performer and the listener.

The expectations of the listener depend on a number of considerations, but audiences generally seek an expressive performance, which demands reasonable accuracy, presented with spirit, ease, and conviction. The performer's expectations are also quite complex, but there is one in particular that is often overlooked: the performer's need to enjoy performing. To do this, one must not only engage with the music, but also have confidence that one will perform well every time. This confidence comes from a deep sense of security—a complete trust in one's ability to achieve a high standard of playing in each performance.

The main impediment to this kind of performing can often be attributed to "performance anxiety" or "stage fright." When severe, this condition can be incapacitating—but even when mild it is an unpleasant hindrance. The causes of performance anxiety may seem elusive, but the problem is so pervasive that it is frequently the topic of books and articles. Wide-spread performance anxiety results from fear of failure and the resulting humiliation. Even so, it strongly appears that nearly all students dedicated enough to learn to play an instrument have a natural desire to share music with others, and to earn admiration for their effort.

Unfortunately, many talented students and even advanced professionals are denied such positive experiences because of the crippling effects of performance anxiety. The approach outlined in this method is the product of an effort to eliminate performance anxiety by developing positive performance habits from the very earliest stages of training. The result is effective not only because of the quality or accuracy of the information, but also because of the step-by-step presentation. Information will be introduced only when it is needed and has immediate application. The outcome is a gradual process of learning that leads most quickly to habits of security and confidence, and positive feelings of progress—both essential parts of enjoying guitar study. The emphasis on forming these habits (which are the product of the student's thought process) have prompted a fuller focus on the mental aspects of learning to play the guitar—on the dominant role of the mind. The role of the mind was the primary focus of the *Introduction* in my book *The Shearer Method Classic Guitar Foundations* and will remain a thread of continuity throughout this book and the entire series.

ABOUT THIS BOOK

This book continues the technical and musical development begun in Book 1—*The Shearer Method: Classic Guitar Foundations*. Material in the present text assumes mastery of foundations, such as proper positioning, free-stroke technique, arpeggios, and music reading. Thus, if you are new to guitar study, it is *strongly* advised to first thoroughly work through Book 1. Moreover, Book 1 lays the foundation for important approaches to study and practice (e.g. *visualization* and *pre-reading*) which are referred to here and in subsequent volumes.

Technical emphasis in Book 2 centers on rest-stroke, scale forms, arpeggios without *p*, shifting, barring, slurs, and ornamentation. Areas of music study include theory, chords, reading in keys and a continued study of rhythm and meter. In addition the book outlines strategies for visualization, pre-reading, and air guitar, ultimately applying these skills to memorization and performance. Finally all of the concepts and technique learned may be further applied in the section at the end of the book called *Music of the Masters*. Here you'll find of a variety of selections from the standard repertoire organized by historical period, including Renaissance, Baroque, Classical, and Romantic.

USING THE MULTIMEDIA DISC

This book comes with a single disc that contains all of the multimedia presentations, both *video* and *audio*. The videos play in a standard DVD player or computer but the audio (TNT2 encoded) *will only* work in your computer. The book serves as the foundation for the method. However, subjects that require clarification beyond the text are demonstrated in the accompanying videos which visually help you to form better understanding. As you work through this book, refer to videos whenever you see the symbol. The concepts involved in learning the classic guitar can often be complex—feel free to review both the text and videos frequently.

In addition, the audio portion of the disc contains all of the duets, and a few helpful selections from the solo pieces. Refer to these whenever you see the audio symbol. The audio plays on any computer using the TNT2 (*Tone and Tempo*) software that comes with the disc. This allows you to:

- speed up or slow down tempo.
- control the volume for each track.
- *solo* the student's or teacher's part.
- turn the metronome on or off.
- loop sections to repeatedly rehearse them.

(See the multimedia disc instructions opposite the media disc pouch.)

ABOUT THE SHEARER ONLINE SUPPLEMENT

The ***Shearer Online Supplement*** at **www.aaronshearerfoundation.org** contains articles that, while providing essential information for learning to play the guitar well, are more suitable outside the present text. Further, the *Supplement* contains articles that, are meant to provide the enterprising student a factual, well-rounded view of the often confusing world of guitar instruction. Thus the text and the *Supplement* are interdependent. The text becomes more meaningful through applying information found in the *Supplement* and the *Supplement* makes orderly sense only when used in conjunction with the text. When you see WWW be sure to visit the corresponding article at **www.aaronshearerfoundation.org**. In addition to the *Shearer Online Supplement* you will find other resources for students, teachers and performers interested in learning more about Aaron Shearer's life work.

POSITIONING REVIEW

Though seating position and hand checks were introduced in depth in *Classic Guitar Foundations,* it is always wise to re-evaluate your seating position on a regular basis. As you learn more difficult selections, you will discover that your seating position might need to be refined to meet the challenges that are required in the music. Don't be afraid to experiment and refine your positioning using the videos both presented here and in Book 1.

DAILY WARM-UP ROUTINE

The beginning of *Classic Guitar Foundations* introduced concepts of finger flexion and extension with reference to an exercise in the *Shearer Online Supplement* for muscle stretching[1] In addition, as you learned about objectionable side pull of fingers, the online supplement taught you about a finger independence exercise helping you heighten the coordination of your hands.[2] These exercises will now form the foundation of a daily routine used not only for warm-ups but "cool downs," framing your practice.

All too often students begin their activities by intensely practicing and focusing on musical issues and do not realize that they are reinforcing habits of tension due to not warming up. Just as in sports, athletes warm up muscles first with light activity and stretching before doing any strenuous workout, so should you perform light movement activities and stretches before attempting to play. These activities will help condition and tone muscles in your hands and arms as well as reduce tension that can lead to injury due to muscular strain.

Realize the type of warm-up activity and the duration of the activity is only a suggestion made here as a point of reference. Each individual will vary the type and amount of activity based on their own needs and experience. Listen to your body and if any strain, tension or pain is experienced then stop this activity until you can meet with your teacher and discuss an alternative exercise. There should be NO pain associated with any of these exercises and if pain is what you are experiencing, then seek the attention of a medical physician.

---

1 *The Shearer Method Book 1: Classic Guitar Foundations*, p. 2.
2 *Book 1*, p. 138.

Individual Finger Isolation

The *Shearer Online Supplement* introduced you to finger independence exercises when you were learning to control finger side-pull. This exercise will now be used as a starting point to not only allow muscles to group with light movement activity but also develop coordination for finger independence. Ten to twelve repetitions of each movement on each hand is a good starting point. As you develop fluency, do these movements in alternation to more closely simulate the skills needed to play the guitar.

Flexion Sweeps *i,m*

To provide a slight resistance to your motion and directly simulate the movement executed on the guitar, flexion sweeps are an excellent activity to incorporate multiple muscle groups working together. Since you will be sweeping multiple strings, don't worry about the accuracy of hitting a specific point on the finger or string. Your only concern is pure motion of the right-hand fingers against a slight resistance.

Flexion Sweeps *m,a*

Balance in the hand is incredibly important. Too many students have fluent *i,m* alternations but falter terribly when required to do an *a,m* alternation. With that in mind, just as you have warmed up with flexion *i,m* alternation sweeps, you will also perform this with *a,m*.

Stretches—Left and Right Hands

Establishing light activities and muscle warm up, creates a good opportunity to now stretch both the flexor and extensor muscles. Just as athletes must stretch out before strenuous activity, so will you. Remember to listen to your body, these stretches should have no pain associated with them but simply reduce the tension that you might be carrying in your hands.

Tone Study

The main purpose of this activity is to create positive habits of contact with the right-hand fingers to the strings. A prepared stroke as introduced in Book 1 is utilized to maximize the opportunity to sound the string with the exact finger placement that produces the desired tone.[3] Then as you reinforce this habit, that specific point of contact and the resulting tone will occur automatically even in continuity stroke.

---

[3] *Book 1*, p. 6.

Left- and Right-Hand Coordination

This exercise begins to bring everything together on the guitar; the motion of sweeps, the accuracy and tone from your contact study, and now coordination between the hands to sound notes. The challenge in this is to maintain tonal clarity during the change in rhythm. Don't allow the sixteenth note to become sloppy or muted, so a slower tempo is recommended at first and only increase the tempo when you're satisfied with the resulting tone. Be sure to work both *i,m* and *m,a* with this exercise. Practice with both *free* and *rest* stroke (once learned—p. 2).

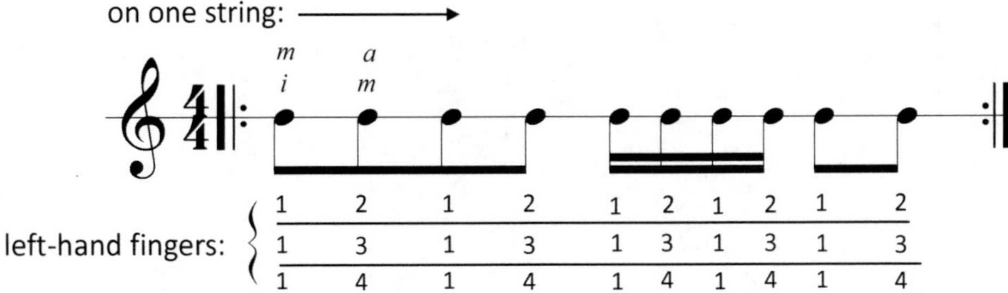

Left- and Right-Hand Coordination with String Crossing

As with the exercise above, a slower tempo is recommended at first and only increase the tempo when you're satisfied with accuracy and tone. Be sure to work both *i,m* and *m,a* as well as both free and rest stroke with this exercise.

Lead with *m*

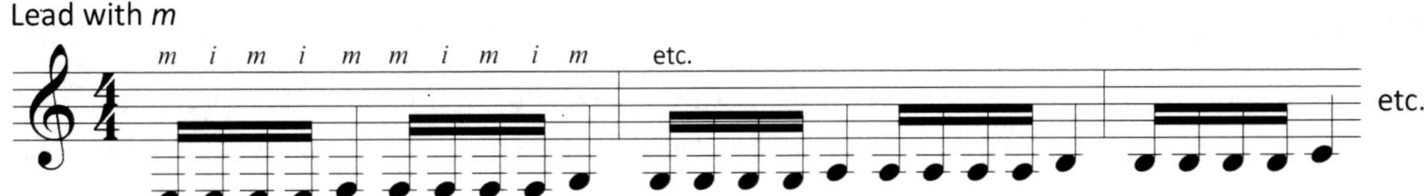

Lead with *i*

Spider Chords

This is truly a challenging left-hand exercise for finger independence in an active playing setting. Work slowly and be aware of any strain or tension that you might feel in the left hand. Repeating your left-hand stretches is a good idea after this exercise.

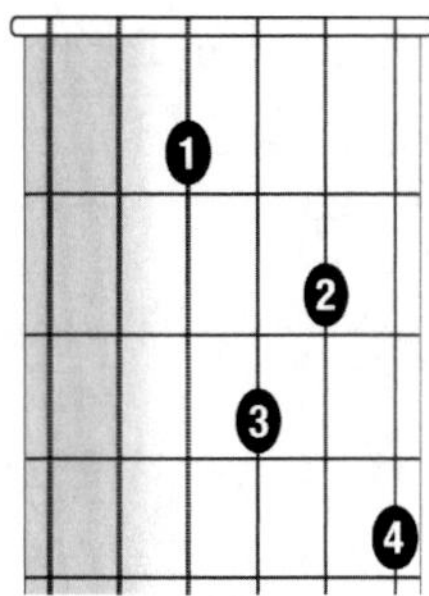

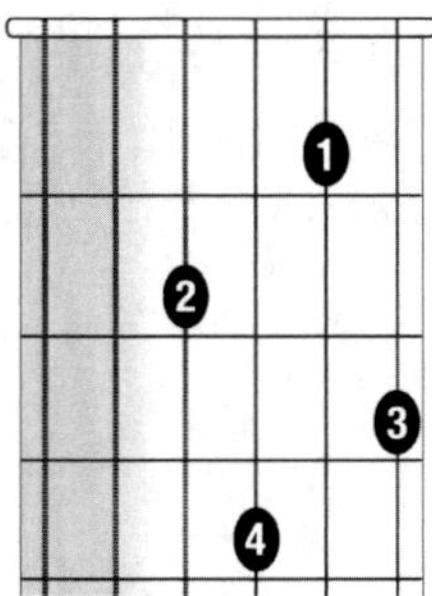

Arpeggios

During your work in Book 1 you acquired a collection of arpeggio forms that will now be used to help the right hand refine its sympathetic motion. Applying these arpeggios to simple chord forms can be a starting point, but applying them to music is the best activity. At first you can use selections found in Book 1; but as you become knowledgeable of the classic guitar repertoire, look for excerpts and even complete selections that use these right-hand forms.

Flexion Extension Sweeps

All too often guitarists focus on their flexor muscle development while ignoring extensor muscles. This exercise will help condition and strengthen both sets of muscles using the guitar string as a resistance. This exercise is saved for last because it tends to present a considerable challenge. If you find that it causes tension, skip over it for now and proceed with the other exercises until greater coordination is acquired.

Closing Stretches

Now that your hands are warmed up, a closing stretch can be a very soothing activity to minimize any tension that might be developing. For that matter, anytime during your practice or life in general that you feel tension or fatigue in your arms or hands, a short stretching session will be a very rewarding activity.

Warm-ups Conclusion

You've now experienced the benefits of a foundational warm-up routine. This routine in its entirety could take up to 25 minutes to complete depending on the duration of its parts; realize abbreviated versions of these elements can be done, creating shorter workouts. As you work with these elements, understand your weaknesses and spend more time reinforcing those areas. Think of your warm-up routine as modules that can be repeated three or four times throughout the day. Initial modules can focus on accuracy and reinforcement of positive habits while later modules can exercise fluency and speed. Work with your teacher to fine-tune and add to these activities.

WHAT YOU NEED TO *KNOW* BEFORE YOU *GO*

Before we begin, let's look over our first selection, *Beginnings,* and take inventory of the skill set required to confidently prepare and play it. Realize that this selection represents a technical and musical baseline for the book. If you're confused, or insecure with any of the skills listed below, it is highly recommended to go back to Book 1 to review and solidify these issues.

Technique:

- *p* free stroke.
- *p-i* dyads, as well as *p-a* dyads. 

- Alternation of *i,m* free stroke in scalar passages. 

- Sympathetic motion of *i, m, a* 

as well as *a, m,i.* 

- Alternation of *p* and fingers. 

- Harmonics. 

(Additional technique not in *Beginnings*)

- *i-m* dyads.
- Arpeggios with *p* and fingers moving sympathetically and in alternation.

Musical understanding:

- Ability to read all notes in the open position.
- Subdividing the quarter note beat and the ability to play eighth notes.
- Ties and syncopation.
- Repeat signs.
- *Crescendo* and *decrescendo.*
- *Ritard* and *a tempo.*

Habits for learning:

- Basic pre-reading.
- Play and Say.
- Visualizing (air-guitar).

Book 2

The Shearer Method
Classic Guitar Developments

Beginnings

Introducing Rest Stroke

One of the central focusses in *Book 1 was* developing a solid free stroke, essential for playing arpeggios and scales. While this stroke continues in the present text, you'll now learn *rest stroke*—a powerful technique frequently used for scales, single-line passages, bringing out melody (with an accompaniment), and general thickening of tone.

Rest stroke occurs when, immediately after sounding a string, *p* or a finger comes to rest against the lower adjacent string in the direction of the movement. In the case of string ⑥ there is no "resting" though the direction of movement is maintained as though a lower string were present.

FINDING THE REST-STROKE POSITION:

- Position the right hand in free stroke position with *p* on ⑤ (to stabilize the hand), and *i* on ④. Make a mental note of the *point along* ④ where *i* is contacting.
- Without shifting your hand/arm optimal position, reach *i* to ②. This is its rest-stroke position. Notice that *i* is now somewhat more extended than when in free stroke.
- Pivoting from the elbow, shift *i* back to ④, maintaining the rest stroke position.
- Compare this position of *i* to its initial free-stroke position on ④ (*i* is now approximately an inch further up the string).

PLAYING REST-STROKE:

- Stroke *i* on ②, flexing the middle joint to move the tip (firmly but not forcibly) toward and coming to rest on the adjacent lower string.
- Make sure the fingertip and nail cross the string somewhat diagonally.
- Practice sounding the open second string, ② with *i* rest stroke using the spoken "prep-play" procedure described in Book 1 to establish a prepared stroke.[4]

Now switch *m* on ①, continuing "prep-play:"

[4] For more on Prep-Play, see *Book 1*, p. 6.

In early practice with rest stroke, your inactive fingers (*a,c*) may start to extend rigidly. This can impede the free flexion of the active finger *(i,m)*. You can avoid this by keeping *m, a,* and *c* slightly flexed and moving along with *i* and by carefully flexing the middle joint of *i* to pull straight back toward the *P-m* joint.

When you feel secure with *prep-play,* practice Ex. 1. Notice the same finger repeats until change is indicated. As before, begin by practicing with added right-hand stability by placing *p* on ⑤. When you're secure, release *p* from ⑤ and practice Ex. 1 with *p* relaxed, lightly touching *i.*

Ex. 1

When you feel secure using *i* and *m* in Ex. 1, repeat using *m* and *a.*

In Ex. 2 involving three strings, the right hand re-positions or rather string crosses from the elbow to different string pairs to different string pairs. Begin by practicing with *p* resting against ⑤. When you're secure, release *p* from ⑤ and practice with *p* relaxed, lightly touching *i.*

Ex. 2

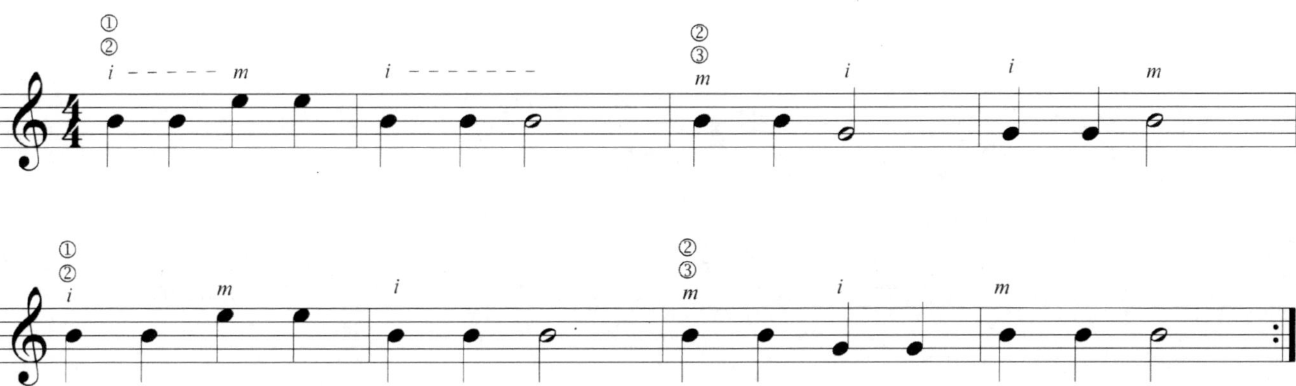

When you're secure with the above exercises begin the next duet, *All Clear,* played with rest stroke throughout. Be watchful for right-hand finger changes. Once secure, practice substituting *m* & *a* for *i* & *m.*

All Clear

REST-STROKE ALTERNATION *I* AND *M* ON A SINGLE STRING

Because the *i* and *m* fingers are of different lengths, rest-stroke alternation on a single string presents a challenge in that, *i* must play slightly extended, and *m* must play slightly flexed. It's important to find a balanced position between these two that feels comfortable and allows consistent, firm, and clear rest strokes with each finger. Be sure to watch the video to clarify your aims:

To begin, proceed as follows:

- Place *p* on ⑤ to stabilize the hand.
- Find your rest-stroke position on ② as described on p. 2.
- With *m* slightly flexed, stroke *i* on ②, flexing the middle joint to move the tip (firmly but not forcibly) toward and coming to rest on the adjacent lower string.
- Make sure the fingertip and nail cross the string somewhat diagonally.
- As *i* comes to rest on the adjacent lower string, prepare *m* on ②. This is the alternation.
- As *m* sounds its string, prepare *i* once again on ② and repeat the sounding of strings.

Practice Ex. 3. When understood, play while watching your right hand:

Ex. 3

As you practice, pay special attention to how each finger flexes and prepares. When finding a balance between *i* and *m,* make comfort, ease, and accuracy your primary goals. Don't neglect the *a* finger: it should remain slightly flexed and moving with *m* so as to maintain the optimal hand position

REST-STROKE ALTERNATION *I* AND *M* ON ADJACENT STRINGS

Playing rest stroke on adjacent strings requires an organization of finger alternation. Just as in free stroke, *m* plays the higher string and *i*, the lower string. Practice Exs. 4a and b—be able to play while watching your right hand:

Ex. 4a - crossing up

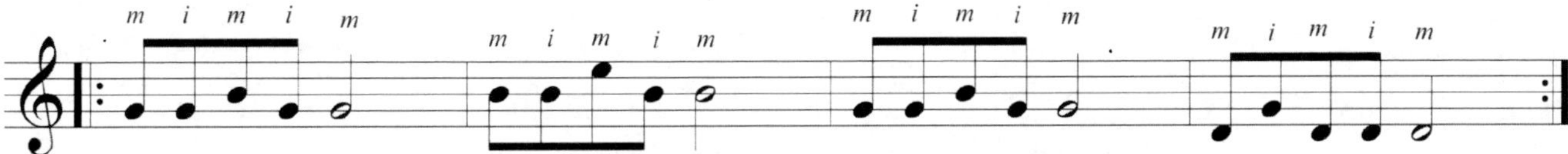

Ex. 4b - crossing down

Another instance of string crossing, the *cross fingering*, occurs where a lower finger crosses in front of a higher finger (or vice versa). This is actually a shift in hand position, where after the crossing the same string continues to be stroked. For example:

Ex. 4c - cross fingering

Practice rest-stroke alternation in the following study. String crossings are indicated by brackets and cross fingerings are marked with (*).

Rest-Stroke Alternation Study

(string crossing)

Visualization

You learned in Book 1 of "Our Four Natural Abilities:" *visualization, concentration, acquiring habits* and *forming aims.*[5] We visualize to mentally prepare ourselves for the musical and technical demands of playing. To assist visualization, we rely on *pre-reading* and *air-guitar* which clarify our understanding and form aims that direct our movement. This is a foundational process that builds images in our minds eye and helps us accurately play a piece of music. To reinforce all of this, the technique of *play and say* solidifies that which was visualized and bridges the mind and guitar.[6]

Habits of Visualization = Habits of Concentration and Movement

Clarifying through visualization is far more efficient and leaves a greater impact than *rote* learning— where the student runs through the piece repeatedly and simply reacts in the moment to the musical notation, making mistakes and then practicing them. In contrast, the process of *pre-reading* and *play and say* is learning through understanding and association, making a vivid encounter that eventually elicits memorization. More importantly while you're doing this, you're strengthening your ability to concentrate and remain focused. This depth of concentration will serve you well not only when you are practicing alone, but when you play in front of others, be it friends, a teacher in a lesson or ultimately on stage in front of an audience.

ADVANCED PRE-READING

As you begin to study more advanced music the *pre-reading* process must become a habit of good practice. All of the following principles are the same as those introduced in Book 1, though organized here in five steps. As always it is important to pre-read only one line or phrase at a time to avoid confusion or error.

Step One— Scan for challenges

Put the guitar aside and carefully scan the piece for unfamiliar rhythms/pitches that may be confusing. For each problem found, acquire a thorough understanding before going on. If the scan reveals many such problems, the piece is probably too complex for you to approach at this time. It's far better to choose material that appears to be a little too easy than a little too hard.

Step Two: Clarifying Rhythms

Beginning with this step we work in small segments. A segment can be as short as a few measures or a small phrase or as long as eight measures; what matters is that it is not too much information as to cause confusion or error. Count aloud and gently clap each note while lightly tapping each beat with your foot to maintain a steady pulse (choose as slow a tempo as necessary).

---

[5] *Book 1,* Preface p. xv.
[6] *Book 1,* p. 10.

Step Three: Clarifying Pitches

Continuing to work one segment or phrase at a time, visualize the notes by saying the string, fret or finger names out loud. For example, A (*La*) may be identified as ③ at II with 2.

Step Four: Clarify right- and left-hand requirements

- *Play right hand only*. As you pre-read, determine which strings and right-hand fingers are required. With the guitar in hand perform the passage on all open strings. Vocalize the right-hand finger name if helpful.
- *Vocalize and touch the left hand only*. Working one segment or phrase at a time, realize the left-hand requirements. Touch and rhythmically vocalize the notes. Say or sing the note names while clearly visualizing where each note is located on the guitar.

Step Five: Air-Guitar

Putting the guitar aside, perform the air-guitar on the same segment while vocalizing the music. Notice how this activity brings all elements of the prior steps together. You're saying or singing syllabic cue, in rhythm while executing movement with both your left and right hands. Free from the physical distraction of the guitar, the fingerings of both hands are clarified in your mind and formed on your hands.

The following illustrates how pre-reading can be carried out on an eight-measure phrase taken from your next duet, *Journey* (p. 12).

Step I — Scan (with the guitar aside)

Step II — Clarify Rhythm — Count and Clap

Step III — Clarify Pitch —Vocalize

Step IV—Clarify right- and left-hand requirements (with guitar in hands)

Temporarily realize the passage as open strings, playing right hand only:

...next, say note names or left-hand finger numbers and touch with only the left hand.

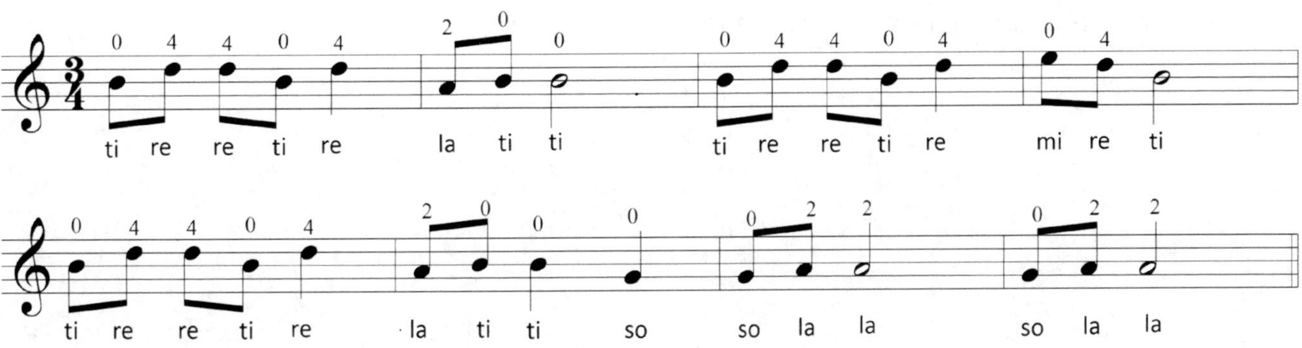

Step V—Air Guitar (without guitar in hands)

This is the culminating moment in pre-reading, vocalizing notes while moving your hands in the air. Each note name serves as a syllabic cue that, with practice, prompts an instant visualization of the other four pre-reading steps. Your ultimate aim should be to form a clear mental image of *all* elements of basic visualization:

- note-name
- string
- location
- both left- and right-hand fingering
- rhythmic function, by stating the syllabic name of the note aloud

Thus, saying "la" should prompt an instant mental image of ③ at II with 2 sounded by *i,* plus its rhythmic function. Watch the video associate with this activity and make sure your air-guitar is allowing you to securely see this information in your mind's eye.

PLAY AND SAY WITH THE MUSIC

Immediately after pre-reading a segment of music, it's essential that you *play and say* it. The activity directly applies all your visualization and brings it to life on the guitar with the added senses of touch and sound. If certain spots in the music are still confusing, then isolate them with further *pre-reading*, or make your segment smaller so as to not have too much information. Many times it takes a few sessions of both *pre-reading* and *play and say* to begin feeling comfortable with a segment. Don't be anxious; take your time, and pay attention to how you feel. If you executed the information correctly but felt overloaded and uneasy, then more reinforcement is needed before going on to the next segment.

COMBINING SEGMENTS

Once you feel comfortable with your first segment then progress to the next applying *pre-reading/play and say*. When two segments are secure, combine them in sequence just as the music would flow and again, *pre-read /play and say*. Go slowly, try to minimize your errors, and don't be afraid to pause to clarifying anything confusing. When you feel comfortable, add a third segment, once again repeating the entire process. Continue in this manner until you are at the end of the piece. If you're feeling secure, then your final *pre-reading/play and say* will encompass the whole piece in continuity. Remember, if any sections are giving you difficulty, isolate them with added *pre-reading/play and say*.

THIS PAGE LEFT INTENTIONALLY BLANK

The following duet, *Journey* should be played with rest-stroke alternation throughout. Your first phrase should now be secure. Approach the remainder of the piece, applying the same advanced pre-reading practice to all phrases.

26
m
i
m
i
m
i
m
i
m
i
i
m
i
m
i
m
i
31
m
i
m
i
m
i
a tempo
m
i
p
i
m
a
mf
36
i
m
i
i
m
m
i
m
i
i
m
i
m
41
i
1.
45
2.
rit. . . . .
p

MEMORIZING MUSIC

After finishing Book 1, *pre-reading, air-guitar* and *play and say* have hopefully become habits, used to prepare music, even if not intending to memorize it. The tools presented in this book, however, are intended to aid and develop memorization. This is not to say that memorization must be carried out with each piece before going onto the next; rather, when you decide to memorize a selection, your goal will be accelerated. Too often students state their goal as to simply *play* a piece. With *pre-reading/play and say* the student works in a logical sequence: *understand* the piece, *play* it securely, and ultimately *memorize* it.

To memorize well, it's helpful to be aware of musical information on a broader level. In addition to clarifying individual notes and rhythms, it's important whenever possible to recognize larger musical patterns, be they chords or melody. For example, an arpeggiated passage may also be understood and visualized as a progression of chord shapes. Recognition of those shapes helps to organize your thoughts:

Ex. 5a

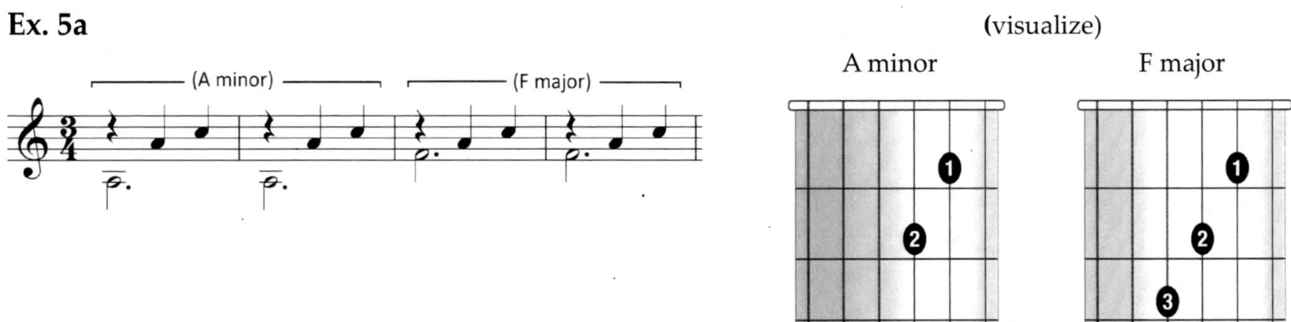

Sometimes music may unfold into patterns called *sequence*, where a melodic idea moves up or down a step which each repetition:

Ex. 5b

Recognizing chordal or melodic patterns aids memorization in that we begin to see the relationship and connection of individual notes. It is analogous in language to recognizing words, rather than individual letters.

Formal Structure

As directed above, always apply pre-reading one segment, line or phrase at a time—but what is a *phrase* and how many phrases are in a piece? These questions address a second aspect of memorizing music—understanding the *formal structure.*

All music has some kind of form generated by a universal need for *repetition* and *contrast*. Music must *repeat*, to provide balance and grounding and must *contrast* to provide change and a sense of progression. Most importantly, repetition and contrast form the basis of *phrases*. Consider the following excerpt from *Etude Antique*:[7]

The excerpt is understood as two eight-measure phrases, defined by a rhythmic pause at the end of each. Compare and contrast the two phrases. Notice the first is almost an exact duplication of the second, except for a difference at mm. 11-12—hence repetition and contrast. To indicate both sameness and difference, the first phrase is labeled **A**, and the second is **A'** (a phrase, similar but different from both of these, would be **A''**). Following **A** are contrasting **B** and **C** phrases, a return to the **A**, as well as a **Closing** phrase (see p.17). Being aware of this order organizes our pre-reading, clarifies the structure of the piece, and facilitates our thoughts for memorization.

TESTING YOUR MEMORY

Consider how *pre-reading* and *play and say* set the stage for memorization. These processes have helped you form and clarify your aims which are now directing your movements—*aim directed movement* (ADM).[8] After a period of time and numerous repetitions you might notice that you're looking at the neck of the guitar more and only glancing back at the music as if it were a cue card. This is ADM at work. Your memory for this selection has started to take root and it is at this time that *testing* should be done.

Proceed as demonstrated in the video and look over the initial short segment that you worked on. Review it with the intention that you're about to test your memory on that segment. Verify that what's in your head is on the page. Then without the guitar or looking at the music, air-guitar and say your syllabic cue out loud as your ADM guides you. Close your eyes if necessary, but proceed slowly and only go at the rate that you see the images in your mind. If you need to pause to see a part of the segment, then do so; but remember to resume exactly where you left off—NO GOING BACKWARDS TO RESTART. Music always moves forward and so should you. If you need to occasionally glance back at the page to verify your accuracy, then do so, but frequent hesitation is the sign that more reinforcement is necessary. After successfully testing your memory with air-guitar then proceed to the next step of *Playing From Memory.*

---

[7] *Etude Antique is* from *Book 1*, p. 76.
[8] *Book 1*, p. xv.

PLAYING FROM MEMORY

Now comes the fruit of your labor. Immediately after testing your memory, pick up the guitar and slowly *play and say* from memory the segment you are working on. Play slowly. If the segment has been prepared well, then your ADM should flow smoothly. Again, if you find yourself hesitating then more reinforcement with *pre-reading, play and say* and *testing your memory* is required.

When successful, move on to the next segment and repeat the process. Put your two memorized segments together and continue to "color in" until the work is memorized. Realize that this will not be a linear progression; sometimes large segments will be memorized, other times short segments will prove difficult. The key is to take frequent breaks and consistently reinforce with the prior steps even after you feel you have it memorized.

Visualization and Memorization: Conclusion

Memorization requires a lot of effort and concentration that you might not yet be accustomed to. Be patient with the process. Go slowly and take frequent breaks when visualizing. Just as your muscles grow strong from physical exercise so will your ability to concentrate strengthen from ongoing practice of ADM. Many times you will finish a session feeling positive that a selection is memorized only to come back and find that it has atrophied; this is common and simply means that more reinforcement with both air-guitar and play and say is required. Continue to be sensitive as to how you feel. If you're anxious, feeling overloaded or even if you played the selection correctly but felt hesitant and uneasy, then again more reinforcement is required.

It will become standard protocol when you go to practice one of your memorized selections that you will first go through the entire piece reciting syllabic cues and performing the air-guitar from memory before you actually play it. This clarifies your aims and solidifies the information before executing it on the guitar.

Invariably the question is asked: "Does this mean I will be reciting my syllabic cues in my head when I am performing? No. Long before you are fluent enough to perform your selection, you will notice that syllabic cues are no longer necessary and rather **images** derived from your Aim Directed Movement are now guiding you through the selection.

Through concentration, you will see in the mind's eye where you have to go before going there.

Again be patient, take your time and remember as the old saying was stated in Book 1: "If you think education is a drag, try ignorance!" **Similarly if you think learning to visualize and memorize effectively is hard, try performing with habits of confusion, error, memory slips and anxiety!**

Applying Memorization

Using the tools and method of visualization presented here, challenge yourself to memorize *Etude Antique* on the following page. When successful, try memorizing, *All Clear* (p. 4), *Journey* (p. 12), and *Beginnings* (p. 1).

Etude Antique

Inventions

Throughout this book, each newly learned key/scale is applied to a set of reading studies called *Inventions.* The invention is a duet, primarily organized with high register on the top and low register on the bottom. Both parts are for the student to learn and may be practiced with a teacher or the accompanying disc. There are at least three inventions in each key, in varying levels of difficulty: *easy*, *medium*, and *more challenging*.

It's recommended that *all* inventions be studied and both parts be practiced with the accompanying media disc (see p. ii, *Using the multimedia Disc*). Some remedial students may find the first invention in each new key easy; rather than skipping, use the materials to practice advanced pre-reading and/or memorization.

HOW TO PLAY THE INVENTIONS

Each invention has been carefully fingered to accommodate R.H. string crossings and L.H. legato. Since this may be an issue of personal comfort, there are places where alternate fingerings are acceptable.

The right hand has been realized mainly as alternation of *i* & *m,* played *rest stroke* where possible. Several instances occur where *a* is used to maintain alternation and accommodate string crossings. There are also several instances where *p* occurs such as bass lines, skipping between non-adjacent strings, or passages involving string crossings (Ex. 6a). In these contexts, *free stroke* is always most practical.

Ex. 6a

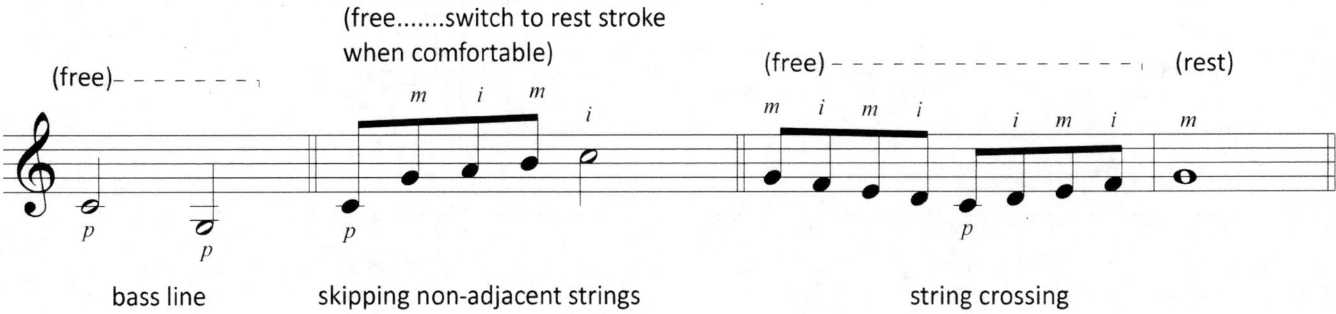

SWITCHING BETWEEN FREE AND REST STROKE

Switching between strokes occurs one of two ways: switching on the *same string*; or switching *between two strings*. Notice in Ex. 6b the ease of moving from free to rest stroke on adjacent strings.

In Ex. 6c, the hand position must be slightly adjusted for rest stroke, extending *m* approximately an inch up along ③ from its free-stroke position. This adjustment is made from the elbow. Do not deviate the wrist when adjusting to rest stroke.

Ex. 6b **Ex. 6c**

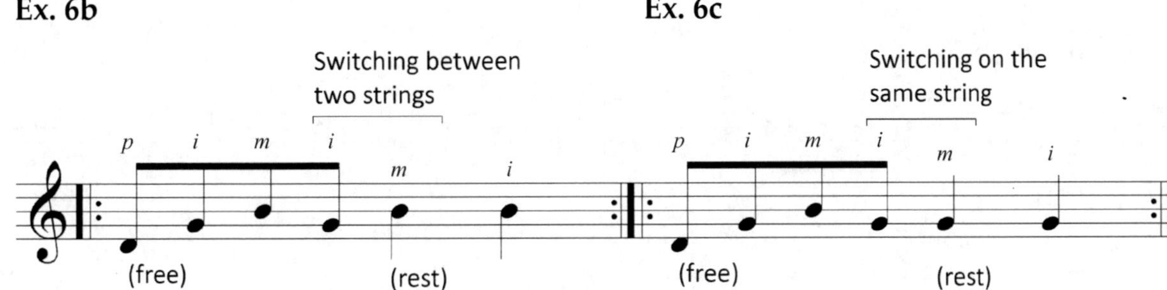

Practice switching between rest and free strokes in the following solo. Be sure to first carefully pre-read. Notice the optional *a* fingering shown in parenthesis at m. 7.

Rest and Free

In the inventions, not all notes will be fingered. In cases where the prevailing alternation is to be continued, only the first few notes are marked (Ex. 6d). A musical segment or phrase that is repeated may have little or no markings, assuming the original fingering is also repeated.

Ex. 6d

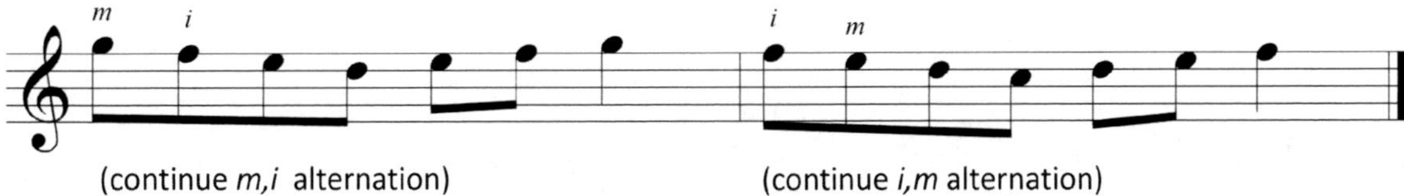

The marking ⟶ indicates to continue playing *p* until otherwise indicated.

Ex. 6e

About The Key

Throughout this book, much of the material is organized and introduced by *key*, so understanding a little music theory is helpful. Book 1 defined *key* as the musical environment which centers around an important note and/or chord (referred to as the *home note* or *home chord*).[9] In advanced music study as well as in this book, it is referred to as the *tonic.* Recall also that the *key* of musical piece is further defined by a *key signature,* a collection of sharps or flats placed next to the clef at the start of each staff. Recall that a signature of no sharps or flats is C *major*.

Scale Degrees

Each of the seven steps of a scale is called a *degree* and is indicated by a Roman numeral. The *tonic,* the first degree (**I**), names the scale, sounding strong and restful. Thus, a scale beginning and ending on tonic C with a key signature of no sharps or flats is called a *C-major scale*:

[9] *Book 1*, p. 71.

Whole Step and Half Steps

Playing the C-major scale on the guitar, you'll notice that not all steps are the same. Some steps are two frets, or a string change, apart—called *whole steps*, while others are one fret apart—*half steps*. Notice that half steps occur between degrees **III/IV** and **VII/I**.

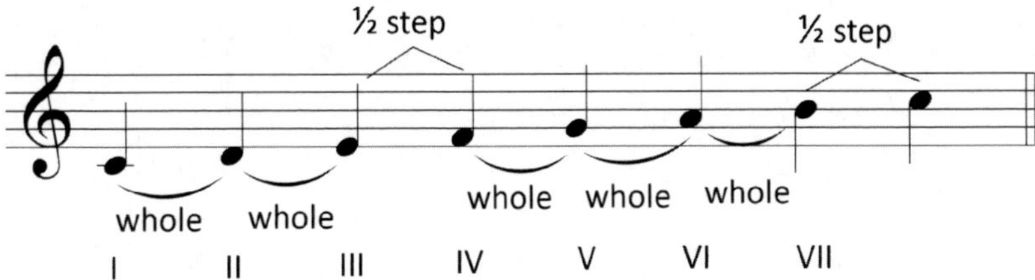

It's important to understand that in order for any scale to sound major, it must follow this specific pattern of steps: *whole-whole-***half***-whole-whole-whole-***half**.

Harmonies

A key is also defined by its *harmonies*—that is, chords that naturally occur within it. Chords built from notes of a given scale will sound natural to its key. For example, consider the chords in the key of C major below. Notice that each chord is built on one of the scale degrees and is each made of a root, 3rd, and 5th.

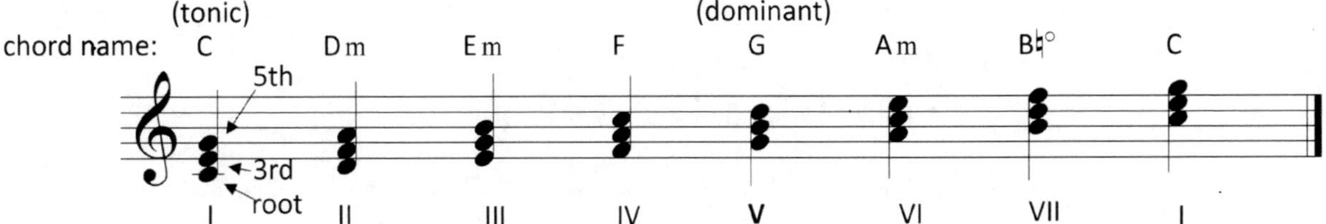

The strongest and most restful of these is the tonic **(I)** C chord played on the guitar as:

C Chord

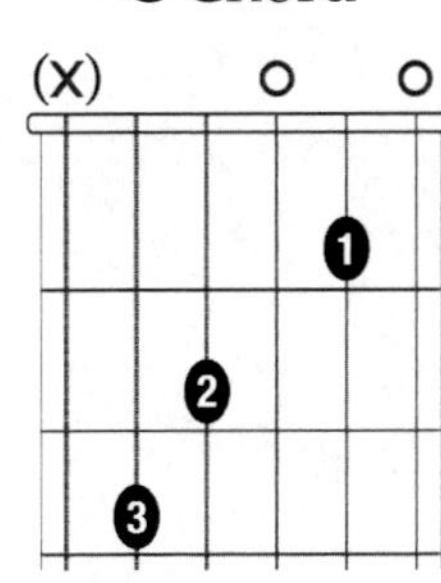

The next most important chord is the dominant G chord, found on the fifth degree **(V)** of the C major scale. On the guitar, it is played as:

(⑤ is muted with the backside of the 3rd finger.)

G Chord

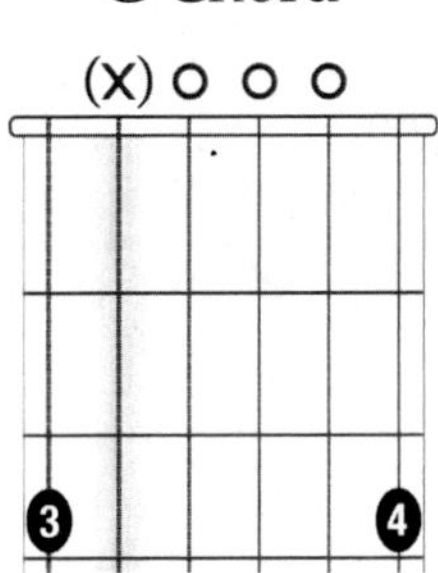

In the key of C major, the dominant often includes a seventh referred to as the $\mathbf{V}^7$, or G^7:

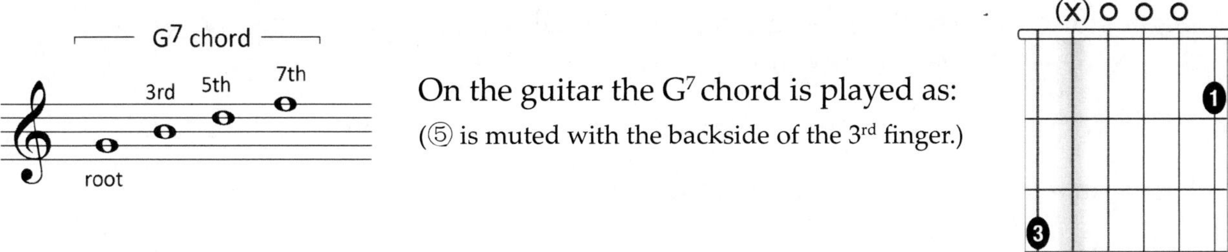

On the guitar the G^7 chord is played as:
(⑤ is muted with the backside of the 3rd finger.)

When played in alternation, tonic and dominant chords create a sense of harmonic progression which strongly defines the key. Strum and listen to the harmonic progression of $\mathbf{I}$-$\mathbf{V}^7$-$\mathbf{I}$ of C major:

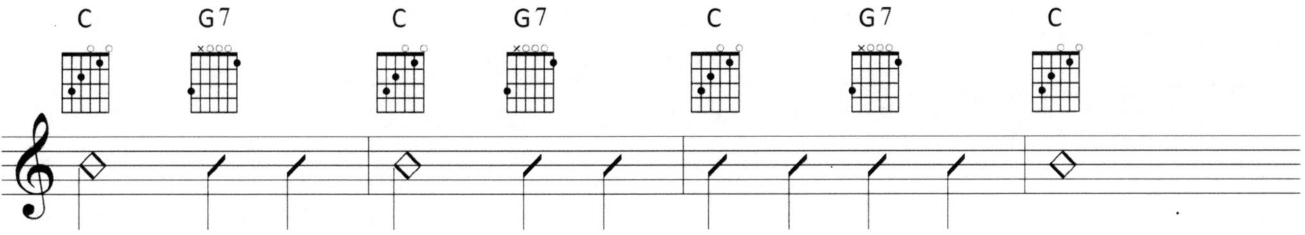

Throughout the book and for each newly presented key, this will be referred to as the *key progression.*

The Key of C Major

Our first key includes all of the natural notes (no sharps or flats) on the guitar, and since its tonic is C (do) is said to be in the key of *C major*. Learn and vocalize the note names.

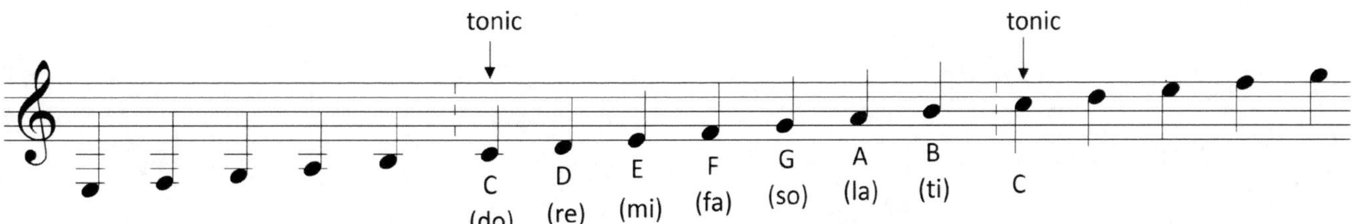

Recall the half- and whole-step order of the C-major scale:

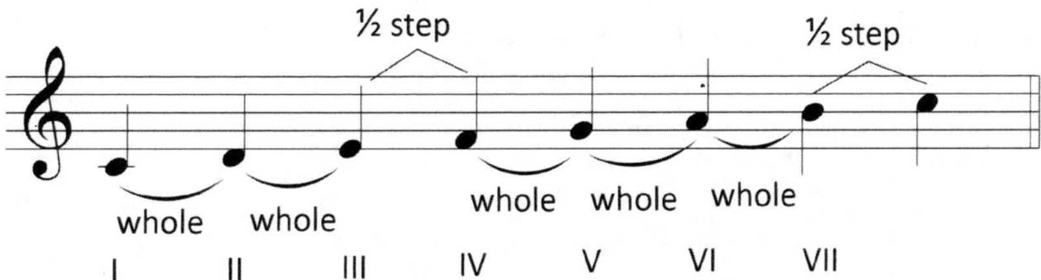

Pre-read, practice, and memorize the following C-major scale. Practice first with *free* and then with *rest stroke*.

- Begin slowly at first. When you can play the scale securely, accelerate the tempo, but continue to play without hesitation.
- When your left hand feels secure, practice the scale while watching your hands.
- Establish a feeling of precise alternation and string crossing.
- Emphasize accurate rhythms and evenness of volume between tones.
- Begin with *i* and *m* alternation; when comfortable switch to *m* and *a* alternation.

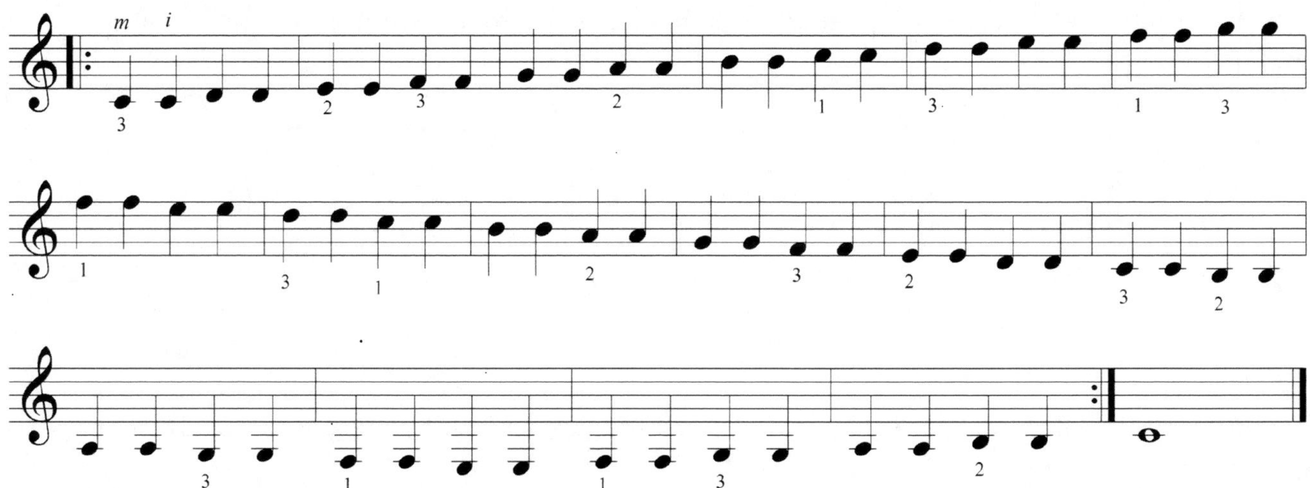

- Finally, when you're secure with the above, play the scale one stroke-per-note, first using free and then rest stroke.

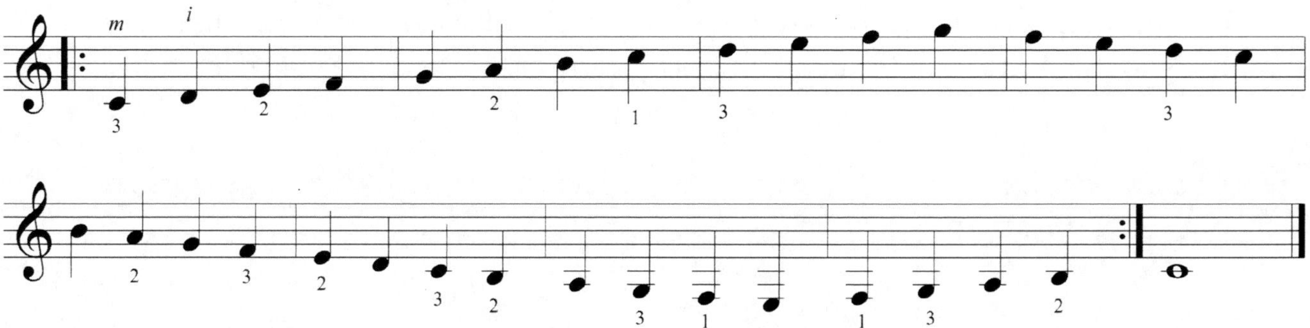

Throughout the book and for each new scale introduced, follow this same procedure. Your ultimate goal should be to play each scale one stroke-per-note, from memory. Remember, always begin *slowly;* accelerate the tempo only once you're secure.

Harmony

Recall the **I** and **V**^{7}chords in the key of C major:

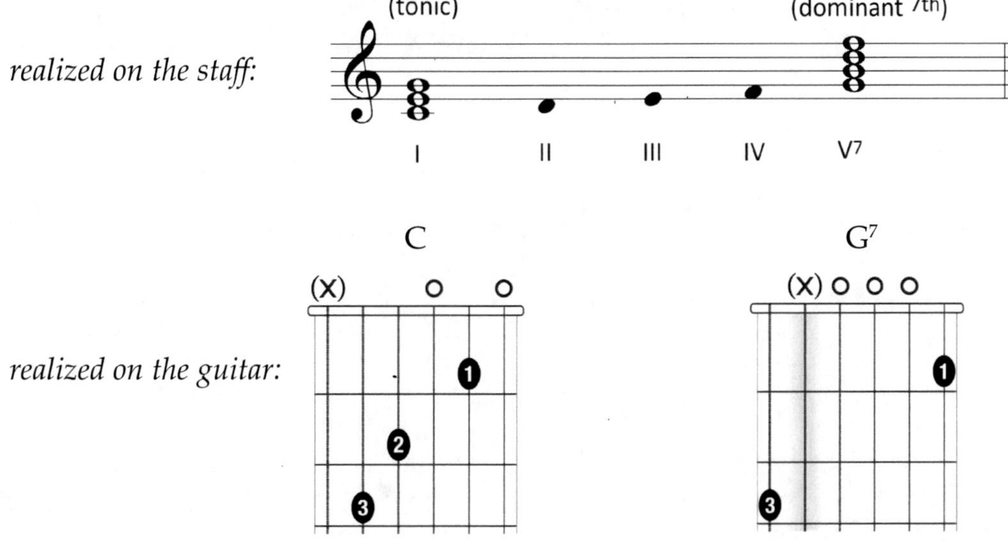

To establish a harmonic foundation, strum the key progression (**I-V**^{7}**-I**)

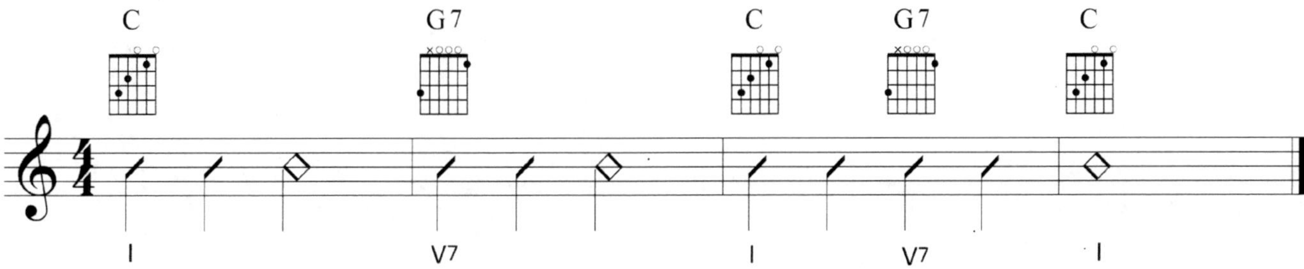

The following inventions will develop your ability to read in the key of C major. Remember to pre-read one line or segment at a time. Practice with your teacher or the accompanying media disc.

Invention in C Major No. 1

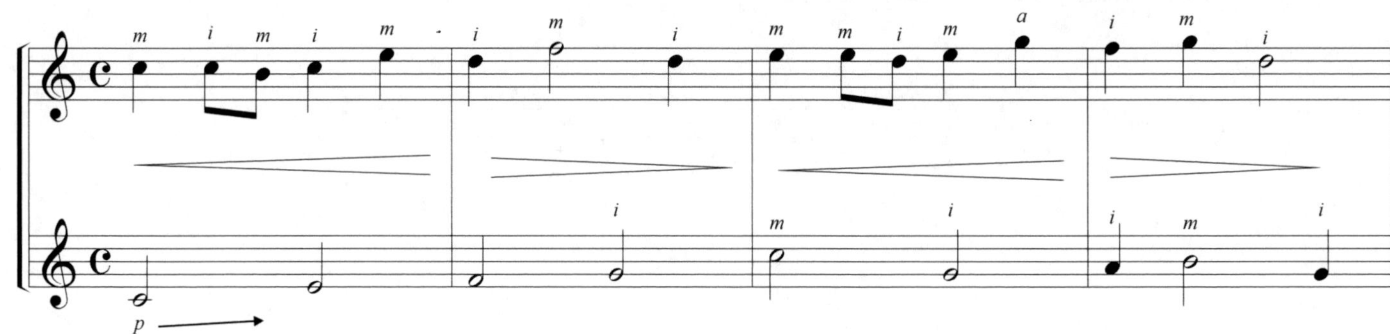

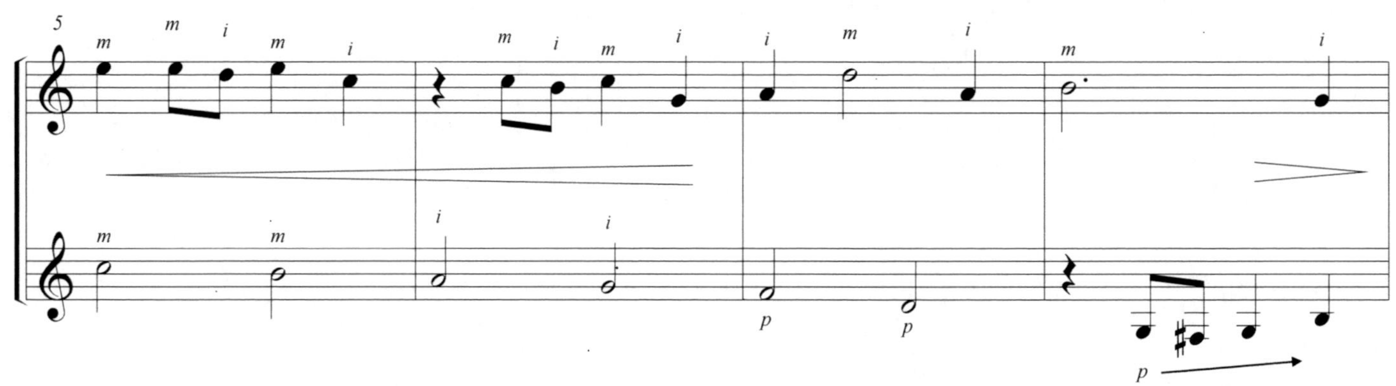

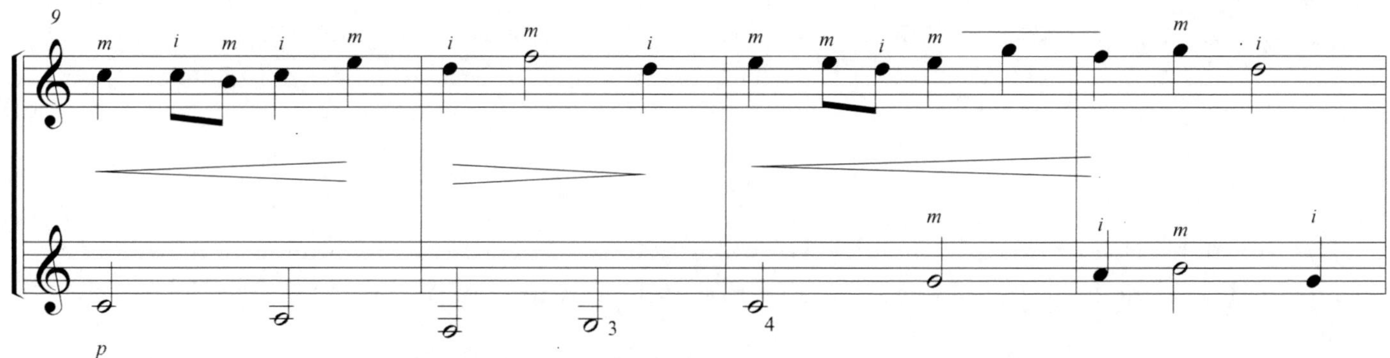

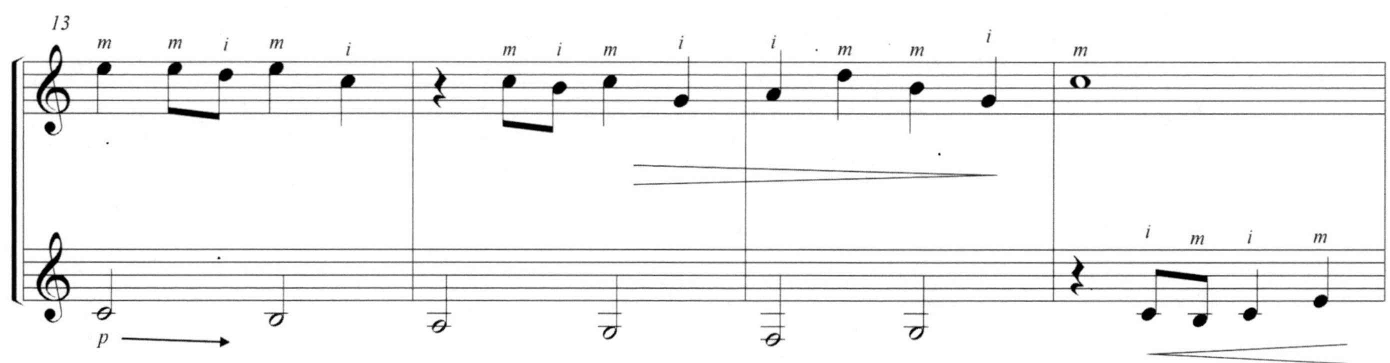

rit. . . . .
a tempo
rit. . . . .
C (strum w/ p)

Invention in C Major No. 2

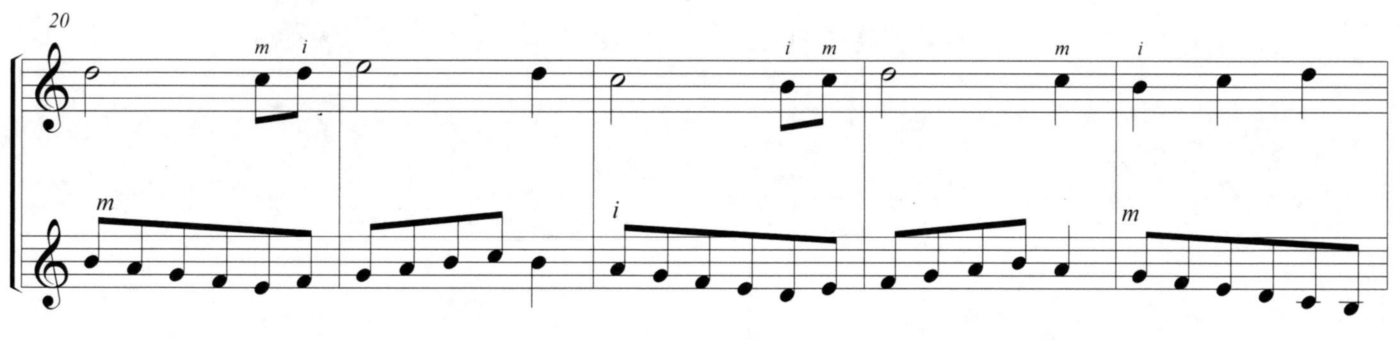
20

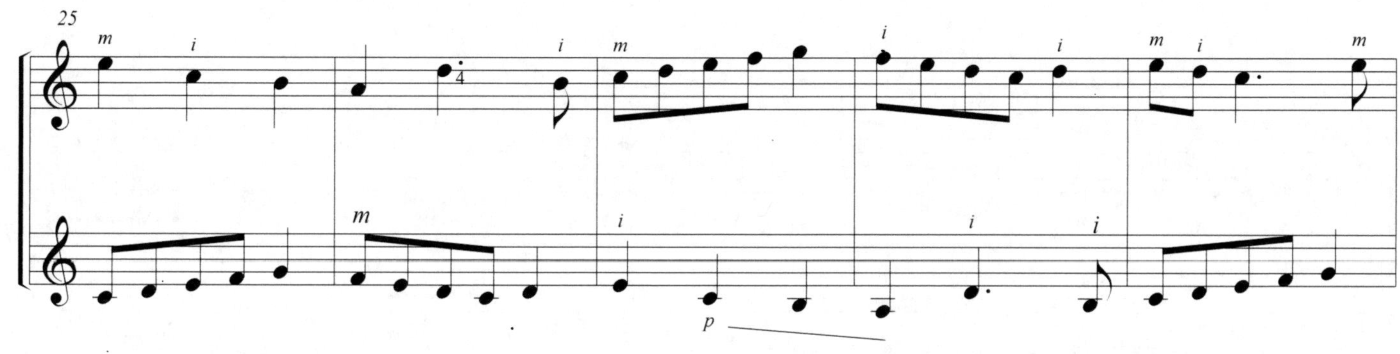
25
p

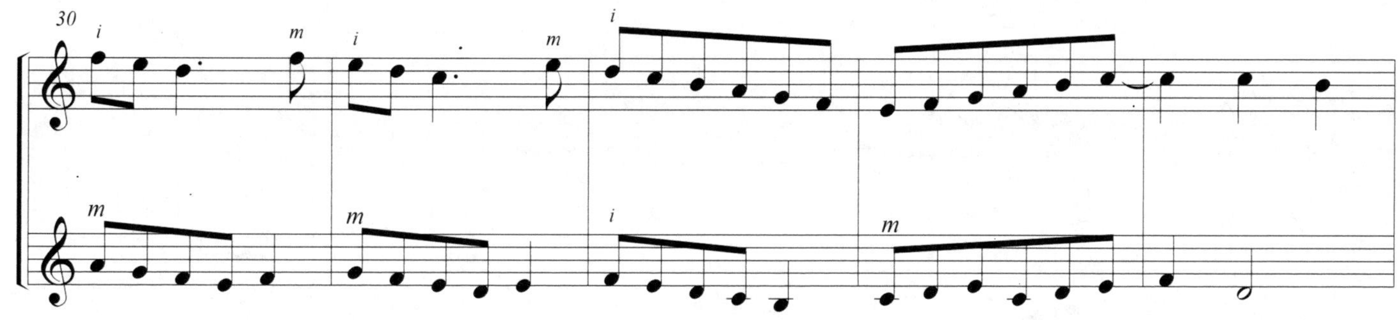
30

35
rit. . . .
p

Invention in C Major No. 3

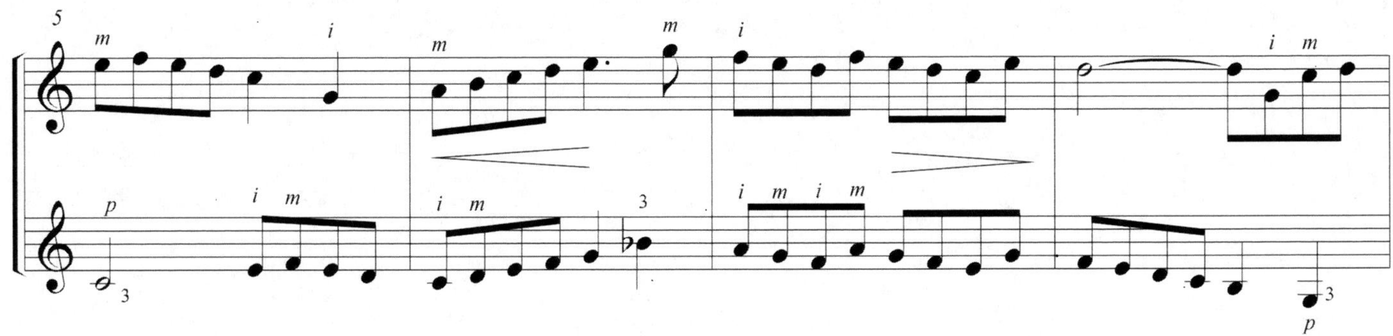

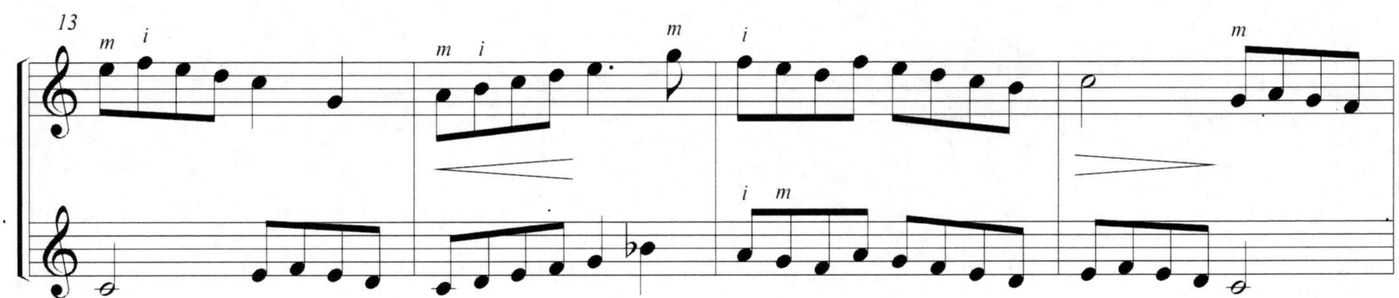

17
21
25
29
1.
33
2.
rit. . . . .
C

The Key of A Minor

Remember that the tonic names the scale. Changing the tonic of the C-major scale to A (la), changes the scale to *A minor*. Compare the following two examples:

Ex. 7a—the C-major scale:

Ex. 7b—the A minor scale:

Because both of the scales share exactly the same notes, they are said to be *related*. Thus, A minor is the *relative minor* to C major; likewise C major is the *relative major* to A minor. *Only the tonics are different*. With the tonic shifted to A, there is now a new pattern of half and whole steps. All minor scales follow this pattern. Notice that half steps are now between degrees **II /III** and **V/VI**:

Ex. 7c

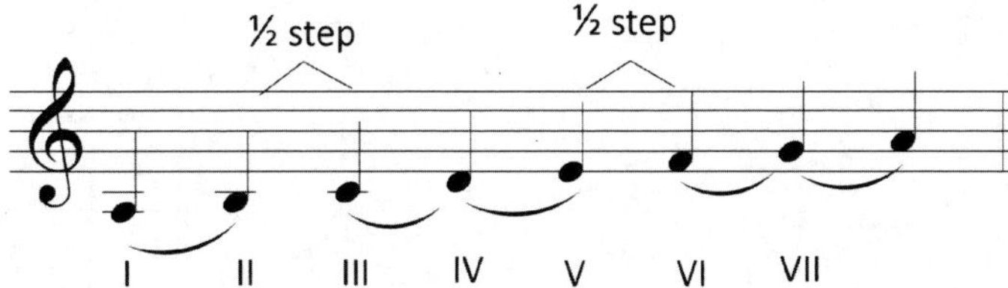

DIFFERENT KINDS OF MINOR SCALES

Since the minor scale in Ex. 7c occurs naturally without alteration to any of its notes, it is called *natural minor*. There are two additional kinds of minor scales which have added accidentals, called the *Harmonic* and *Melodic Minor*.

Harmonic Minor

In natural minor, **VII** to tonic is a whole step which sounds somewhat weak. In *harmonic minor* **VII** is raised with an accidental, pulling more strongly into tonic. As a half step from the tonic, **VII** is now called a *leading tone*. In the case of the A minor, the leading tone is G♯ (si).

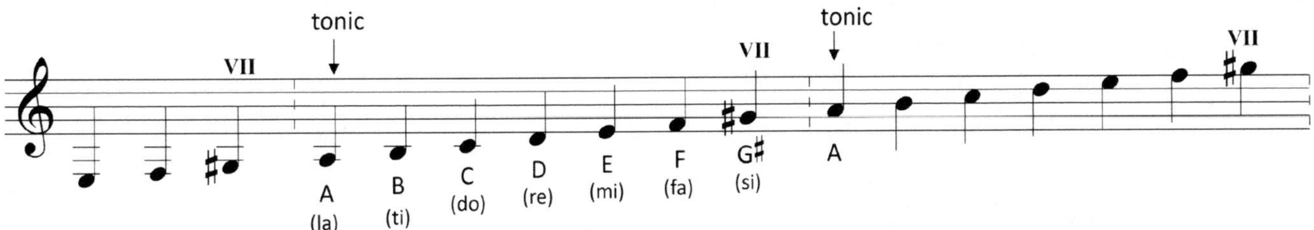

Visualize and learn all notes, then pre-read, practice, and memorize the following *A harmonic minor* scale.

Melodic Minor

Sometimes both **VI** and **VII** are raised as the scale ascends, and lowered as the scale descends. This is called *melodic minor*. In A melodic minor, the raised **VI** is F♯ (fi). Pre-read, practice, and memorize the following *A melodic minor* scale.

Be able to play the harmonic and melodic minor scales, one stroke-per-note from memory.

Harmony

In the key of A minor, the **I** chord is Am and the $\mathbf{V^7}$ is E^7.

on the staff:

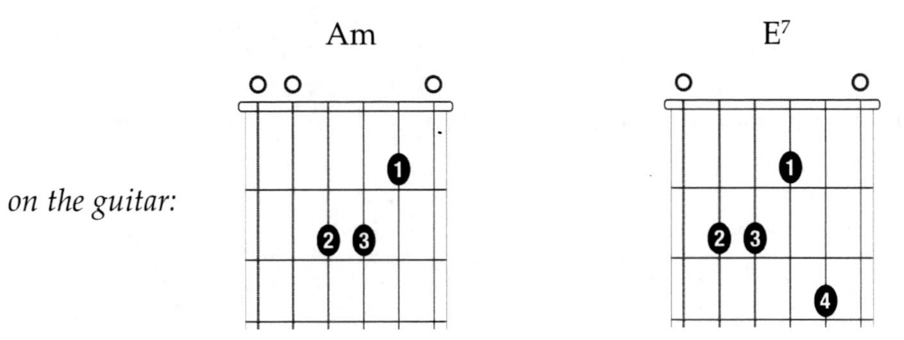

on the guitar:

Practice strumming the $\mathbf{i}$-$\mathbf{V^7}$-$\mathbf{i}$ key progression.

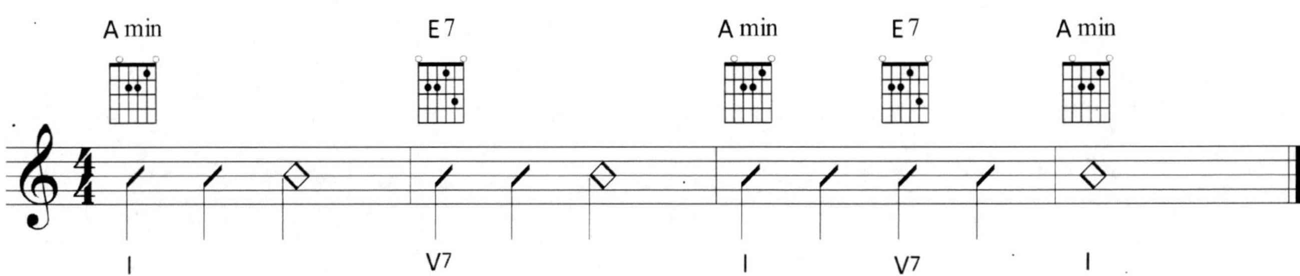

THIS PAGE LEFT INTENTIONALLY BLANK

Notice the G♯'s in the the following Invention—an example of *harmonic minor*.

Invention in A Minor No. 1

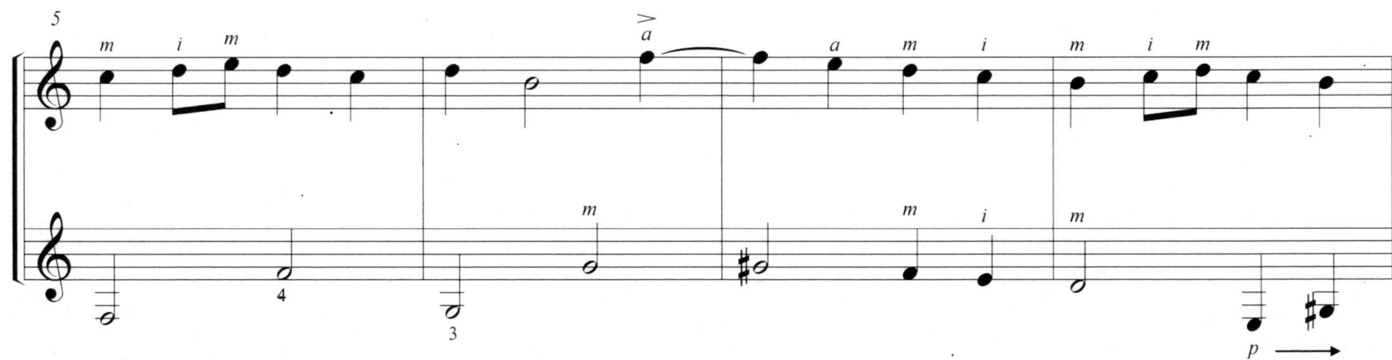

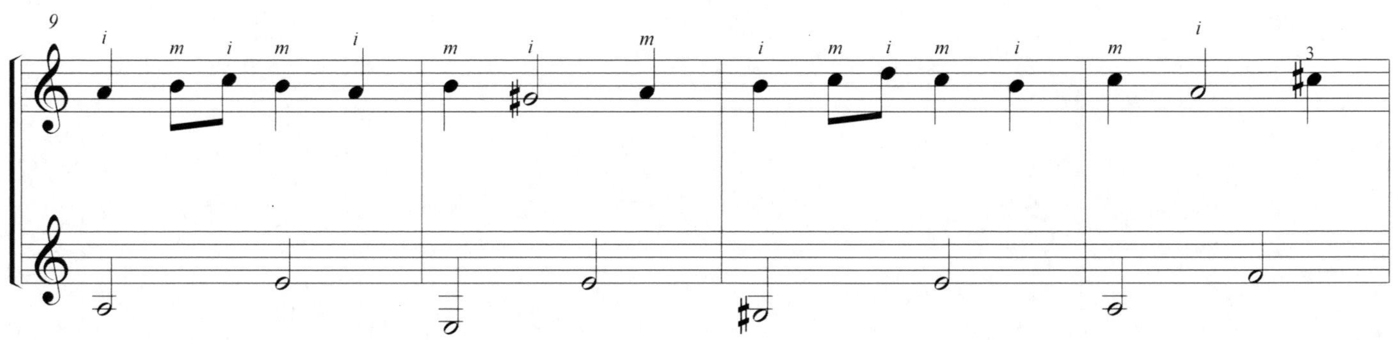

17
m
a
i
p
p

21
i m
i
m
i
m i
m i m i m
i i m
p

26
3
4 –
m i m i
i

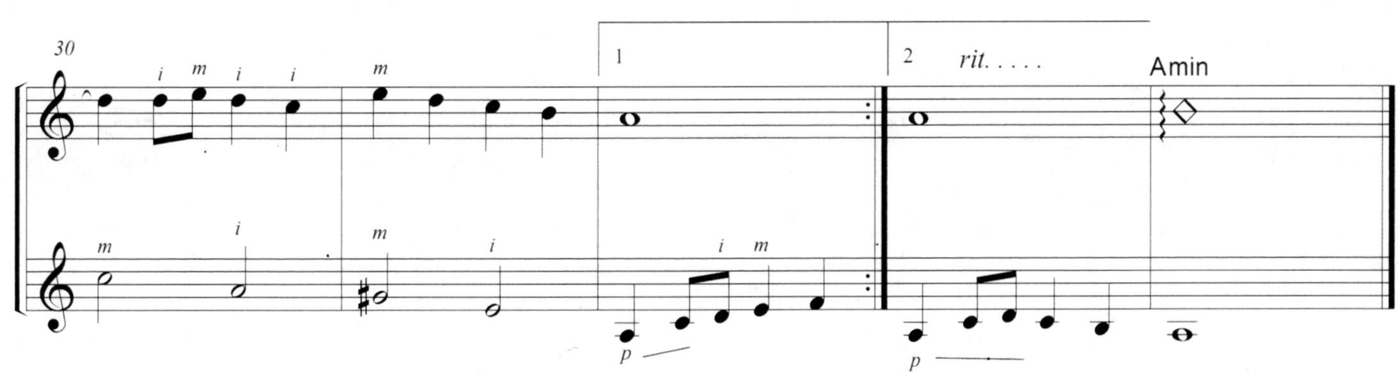
30
i m i i
m
m
i
m
i
1
i m
p
2
rit. . . . .
Amin
p

Invention in A Minor No. 2

When pre-reading *Invention in A Minor No. 2*, observe both the G♯'s and F♯'s. This is *melodic minor*.

Invention in A Minor No. 2

rit. . . . .
a tempo

INVENTION IN A MINOR NO. 3—COMPOUND METER

The meters of all previous inventions have been *simple,* where the beat is subdivided into two's (counted **1**&, **2**&, etc.). The next invention in *A minor No.3* is written in *compound* meter where the beat is subdivided into three's (**1**&a, **2**&a, etc.).[10] Ex. 8a illustrates typical compound rhythmic patterns, including the long-short (L-S) and the short-long (S-L):

Ex. 8a

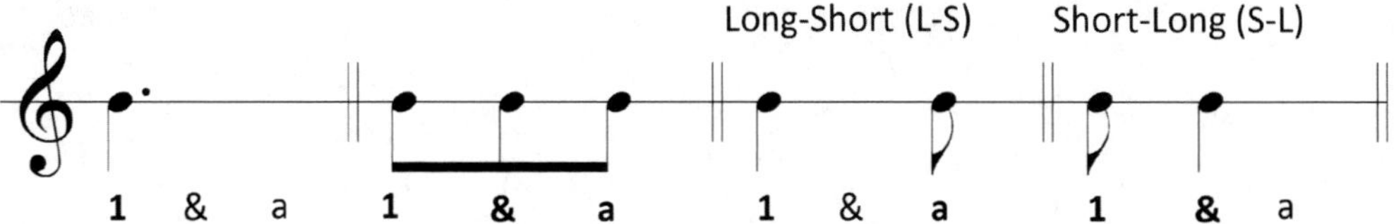

The opening four-measure line of *A Minor No. 3* includes both L-S and S-L patterns.

Practice clapping and counting aloud:

Ex. 8b

[10] For more on compound meter, see the *Book 1,* p. 119.

THIS PAGE LEFT INTENTIONALLY BLANK

When pre-reading, observe both the G♯'s and F♯'s. This is *melodic minor*. Also notice the passage of dyads (Guitar I, mm. 17-27), which is indicated to be played free stroke.

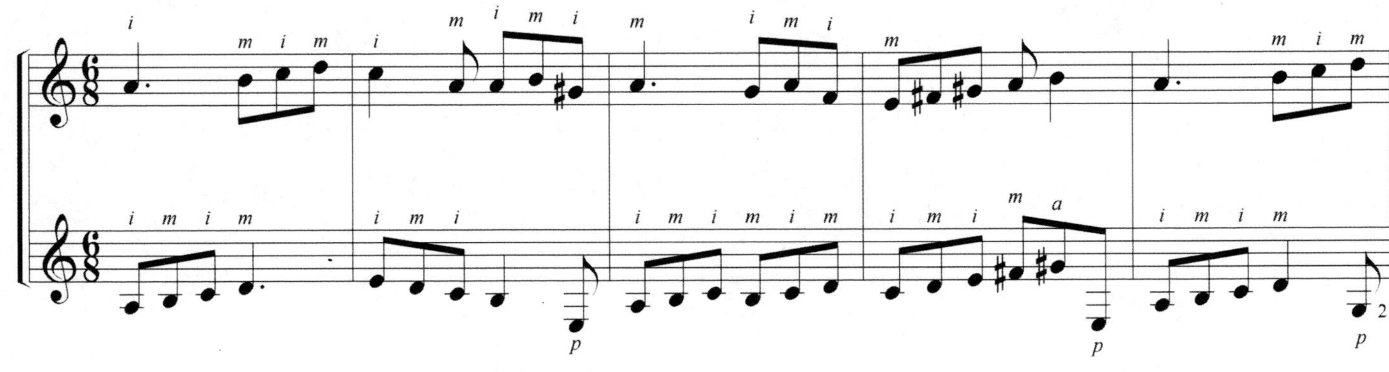

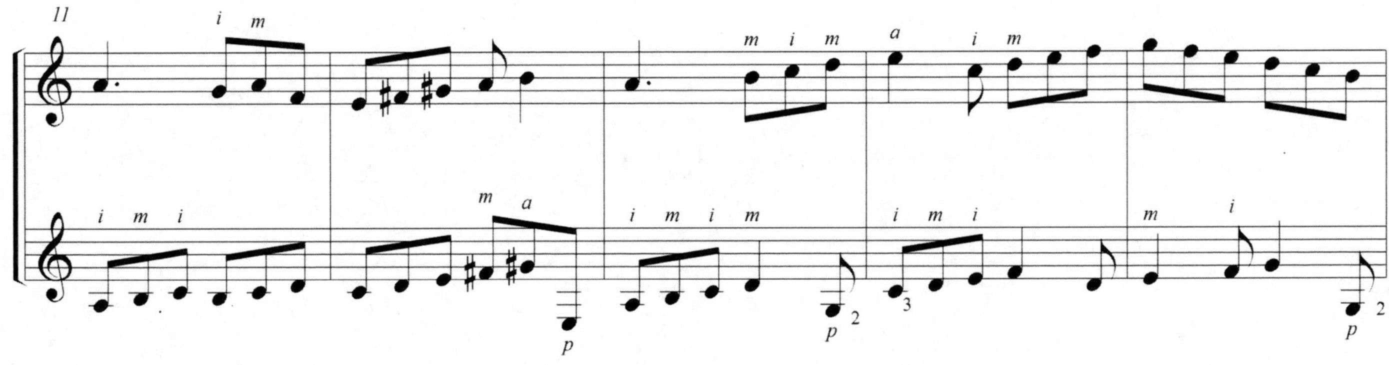

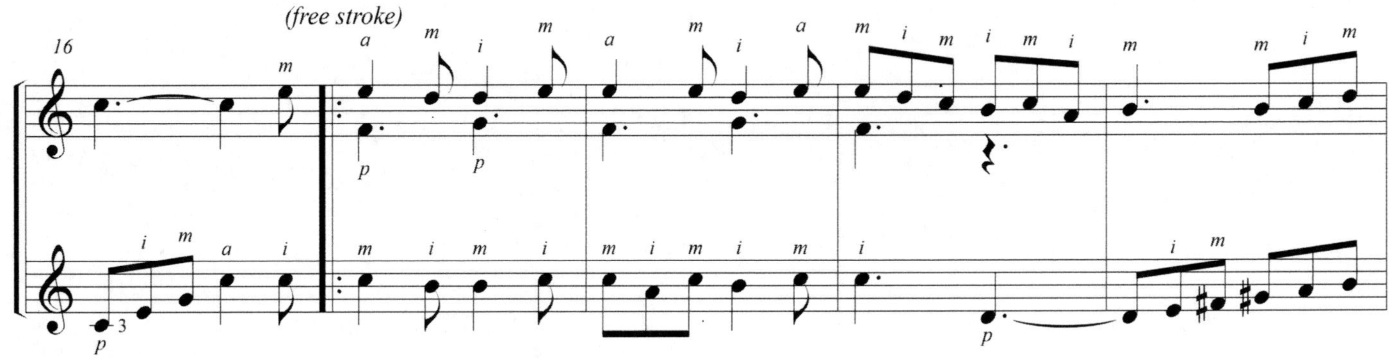

(rest stroke)
(free)

PLAYING CHORDS WITH P AND THE FINGERS

Sounding strings simultaneously with *p* and the fingers poses a unique challenge of coordination. When *p* and the fingers flex together, you may find your hand tends to spring outward from the wrist. If this happens, check to see if you area maintaining the optimal hand position. In Ex. 9, emphasize a steady right-hand position and solid follow-through from the mid-joint, checking that the basal joints do not flex too much (see the video).

Ex. 9

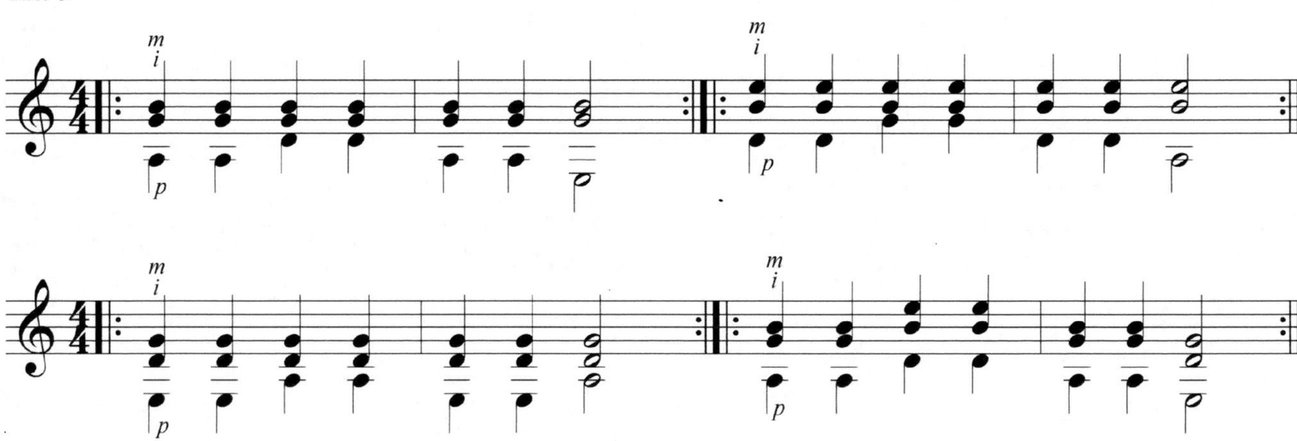

Chord Study No. 1 will help you further develop the technique, while introducing some important common left-hand finger formations. When pre-reading be sure to clearly visualize all fingerings and practice at a slow and even tempo.

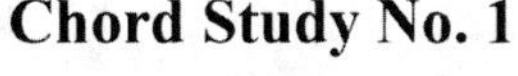

"BLOCK AND ROLL"

Chords of three notes or more may be played one of two ways: *blocking* or *rolling*. *Blocking* occurs when all notes sound exactly at the same time; *rolling* occurs when the notes are played in fast succession, with *sympathetic* motion in the fingers. The effect feels similar to a very fast *p,i,m* arpeggio. Rolling is sometimes indicated with a squiggly vertical line: ⦚ but may also be freely interpreted by the performer.

Practice rolling chords in Ex. 10a & b:

Ex. 10a

When squiggly lines are not notated, performers must decide when to play blocked or rolled chords. CAUTION: too much of one or the other can sound tiresome. It is often best to balance your chord playing with a mixture of both, as in the following:

Ex. 10b

COUNTERPOINT

Continue practicing blocking and rolling *pim* in the next two chord studies. There is an added left-hand challenge in both, where the *p* bass line and *i-m* upper part are sometimes two distinctly different rhythms—called *counterpoint*. In such instances, care must be given to maintain the duration of sustaining lines. This is first encountered in mm. 7-8 of *Chord Study No. 2*:

Ex. 11

To realize the correct rhythmic sustain of the stems-up part, C (do) must not be lifted until the 3rd beat of m. 8. Independence of bass and upper lines is more extensive in *Chord Study No. 3*.

WWW

Great Gate of Kiev

AUDIO 9

Chord Study No. 2

M. Mussorgsky

July
Chord Study No. 3
to JDH
a tempo
cresc. poco a poco
2x rit.

The Key of G Major

Establishing G (so) as the *tonic* changes the key to G major. However adjustment is still needed. The G scale shown in Ex. 12a, is *not* major due to an incorrect order of half and whole steps. Play the following and listen especially to degree **VII**:

Ex. 12a

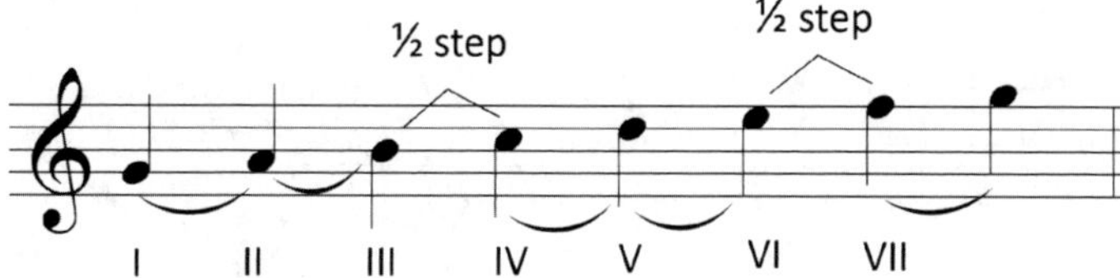

To adjust for a major scale, a sharp must be added to F (**VII**), making it a *leading tone:*

Ex. 12b

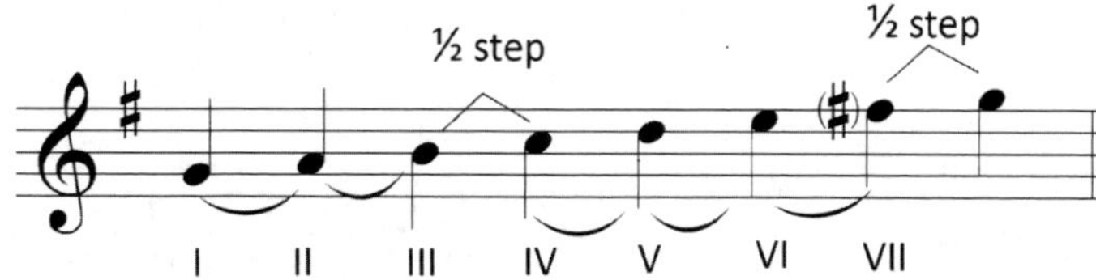

With F♯(fi), **VII** is now a half step below the tonic. To maintain throughout, F♯(fi) is made a fixture notated in the G major key signature.[11]

Review all the notes of the key of G major in open position:

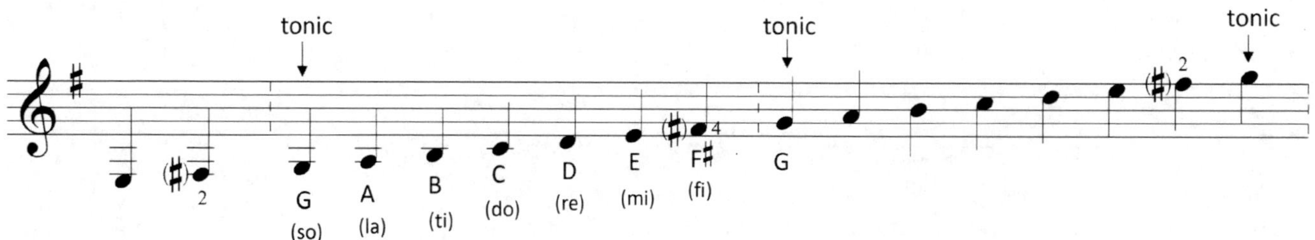

Pre-read, practice, and memorize the following G-major scale. Practice first with *free* and then with *rest stroke*.

- Locate and touch all leading-tone F♯'s on the fingerboard.
- Begin slowly at first; when you can play the scale securely, accelerate the tempo, but continue to play without hesitation.
- Be able to play and say while watching the fingerboard.
- Finally, be able to play the scale one stroke-per-note from memory.

[11] For more information about key signatures, see *Book 1,* p. 71.

Harmony

In the key of G major, the **I** chord is G and the **V**^{7} chord is D^7.

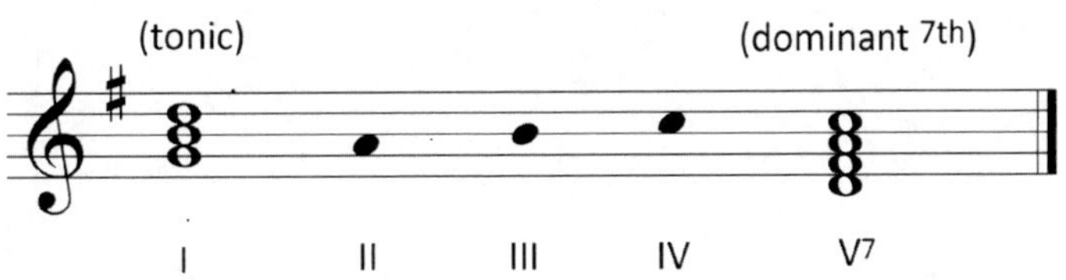

G

(X) o o o

D^7

x x o

When forming G major, dampen ⑤, with the fingertip of "3."

Practice strumming the key progression:

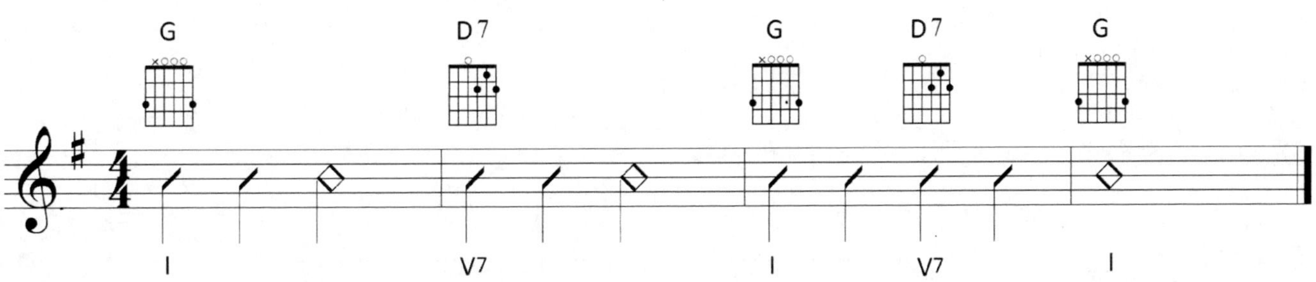

Indefinite Ties

Recall that an indefinite tie means to hold the note longer than its written value.[12] This occurs in for the first time in the following invention in Guitar II, mm. 7, 17, 19, & 34.

Invention in G Major No. 1

AUDIO 10

[12] For information on indefinite ties, see *Book 1*, p. 69.

simile
rit. . . . .
G

SLURS

A slur occurs when two notes are played with only one right-hand articulation. The second note sounds by movement of a left-hand finger. Slurs can be either *upward* or *downward* and are indicated by a curved line as shown below.

Ex. 13

Upward Slur— In an upward slur, the second note is "hammered" on by the left-hand finger, directly behind the fret. The resulting sound comes not only from the string's vibration carried over from the preceding note, but also from the impact of the string against the fret.

Downward Slur— In a downward slur, the second note is articulated by "pulling off" or plucking the string with the left-hand finger to sound a lower note.

Correctly executing a slur requires that the second note sound as loud as the first. In addition, it's very important to play slurs in correct rhythmic context. Beginners frequently slur too fast resulting in a rhythmic distortion. Practice Ex. 14, with steadiness of movement in both right- and left-hands. Set your metronome as indicated or slower.

Ex. 14

Downward slurs of two fingered notes, requires preparation of *two* left-hand fingers on the string. In the following, place both 3 on D and 1 on C, then "pull off" 3 to sound C.

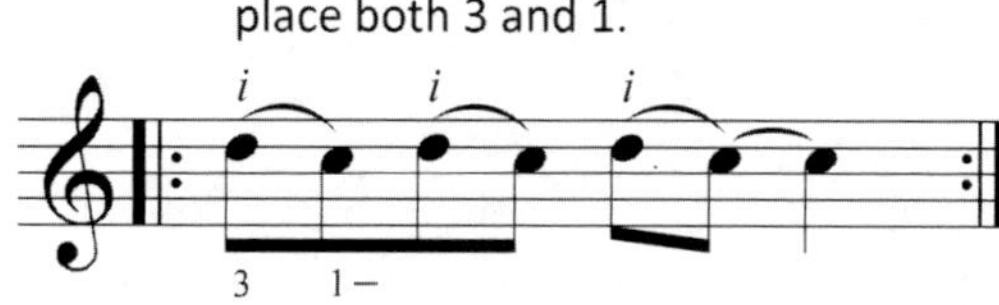

Next, place both 3 on D and 2 on C♯, then "pull off" 3 to sound C♯.

Three Slur Exercises

Ex. 15a—Upward Slurs

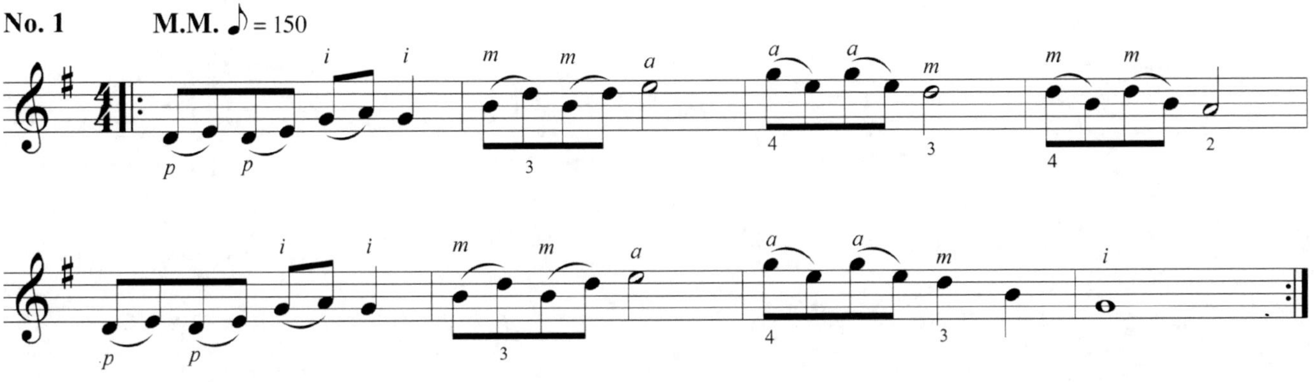

Ex. 15b—Downward Slurs

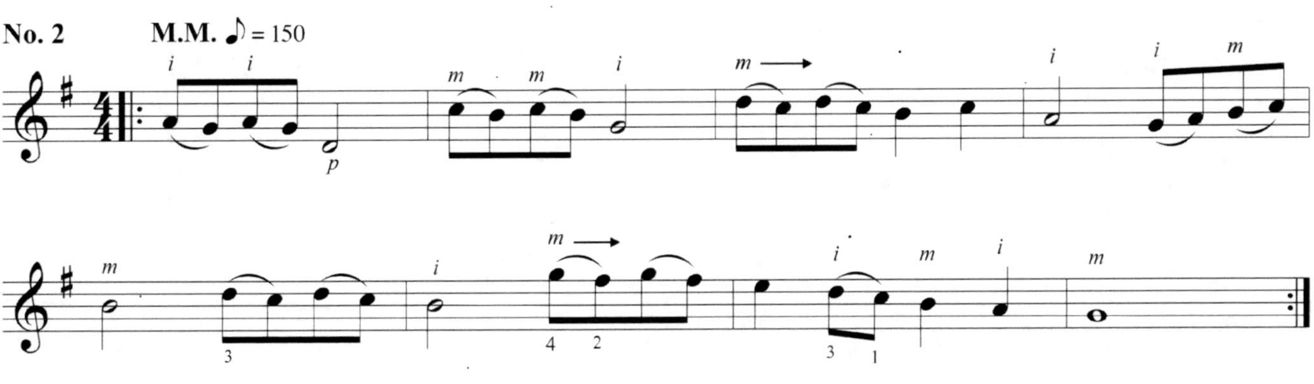

Ex. 15c—Upward and Downward Slurs

You'll find slurring beginning with *Invention in G Major No. 2.* Remember to apply the pre-reading procedures one line or phrase at a time.

Invention in G Major No. 2

17
21
25
29
33
G
rit. . . . .

Syncopation

Invention in G Major No.3 features several recurring syncopated rhythmic figures. Before pre-reading, clap and count each aloud.

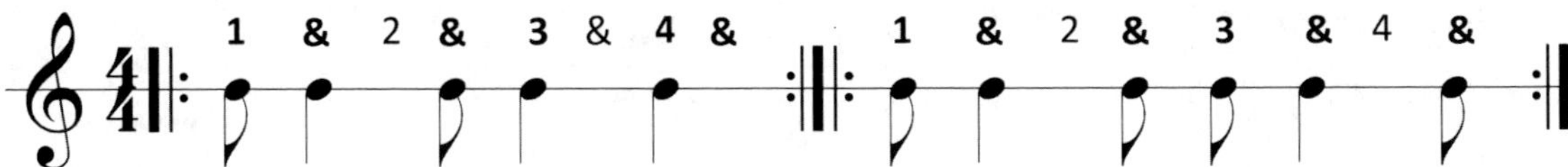

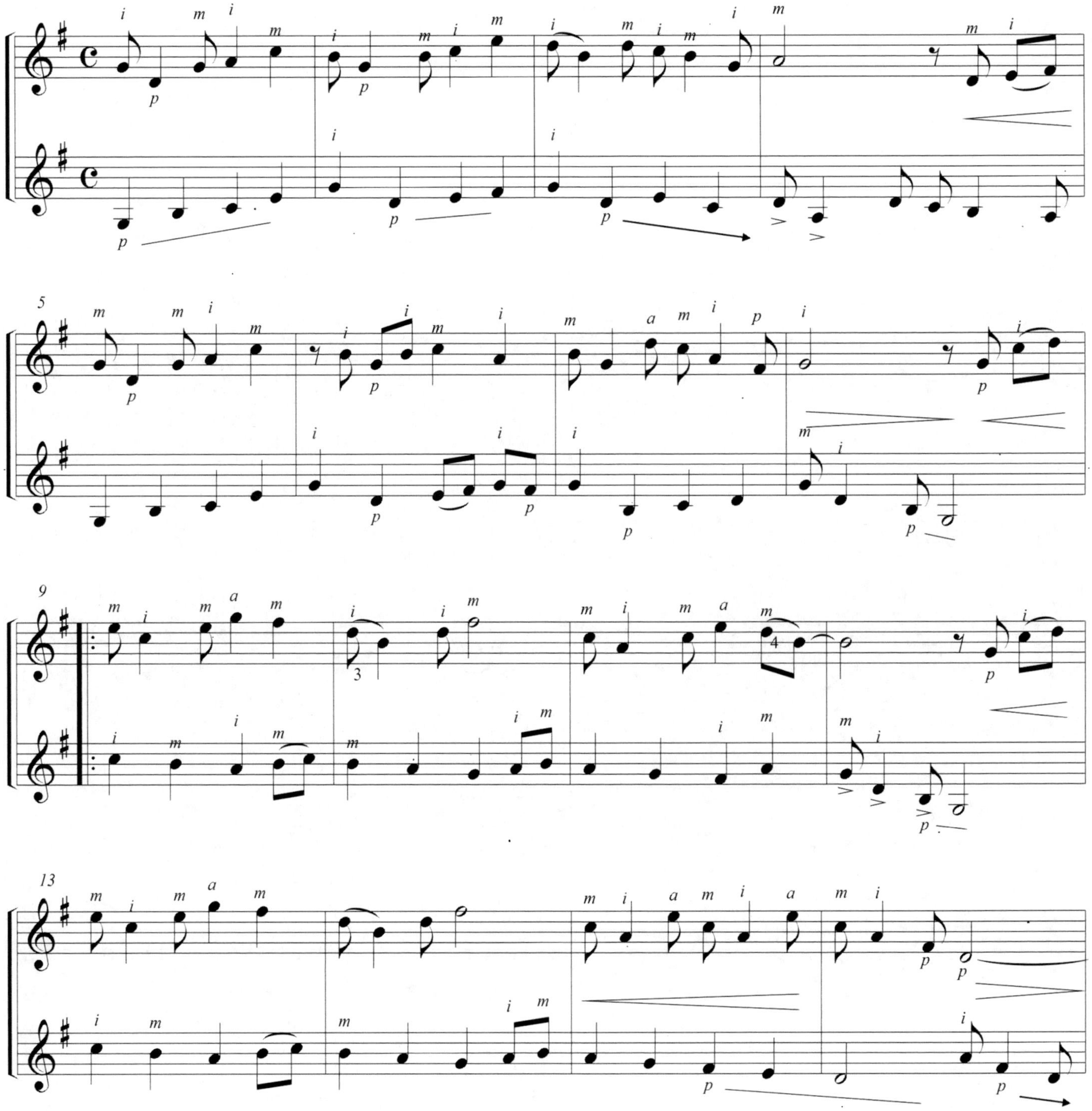

SECOND POSITION

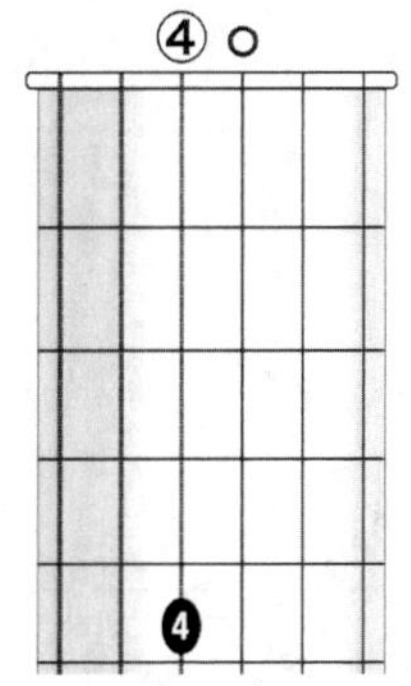

Chord Study No. 4, *Ballad*, provides continued practice with *p-i-m* chords, while introducing a new left-hand challenge. Near the end of the piece, G on ④ at **V** sounds *simultaneously* with open string G on ③:

In order to play, the left hand must momentarily shift into a position further along the neck. By placing left-hand "4" on G, "1" is now oriented over fret **II**. This is called *second position*, indicated by Pos II (named by where finger "1" is).

Establish a sense of playing in second position in the following exercise:

Ex. 16

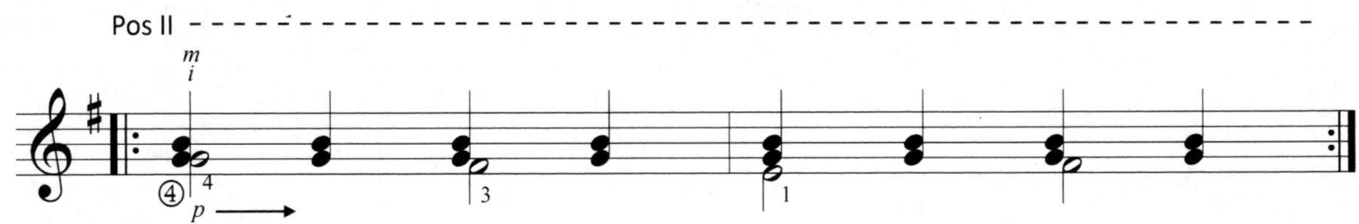

Chord Study No. 4

Ballad

♩ = 110

rit.
a tempo
Pos II
rit. . . . .
Slower

The Key of E Minor

The relative of G major is E minor with a key signature of one sharp (F♯) and tonic E. Below is the scale's whole-half-step pattern, characteristic of natural minor.

E Natural Minor Scale

Review all of the open-position notes available in E natural minor:

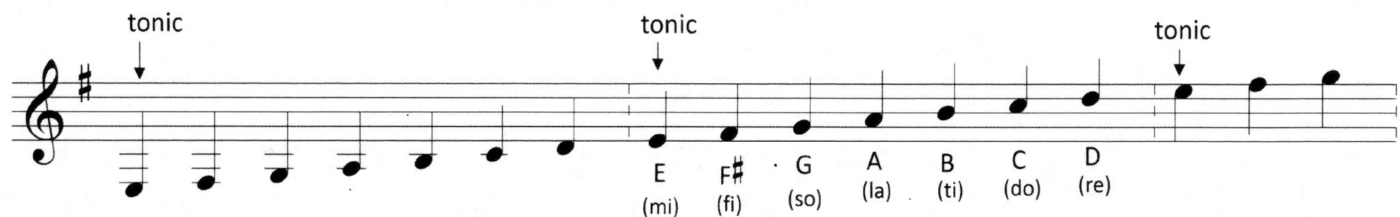

E Harmonic Minor

Adding the accidental D♯ (ri) to E minor creates a leading tone and changes the scale to *harmonic minor*.

Pre-read, practice, and memorize the following *E harmonic minor* scale.

E Melodic Minor

Adding accidentals C♯ (di) and D♯ (ri) raises the **VI** and **VII** degrees, and changes the scale to E *melodic minor.* Pre-read, practice, and memorize the following *E melodic minor* scale.

Be able to play the harmonic and melodic minor scales, one stroke-per-note from memory.

Harmony

In the key of E minor, the tonic **I** is Em and the dominant $\mathbf{V}^7$ is B^7.

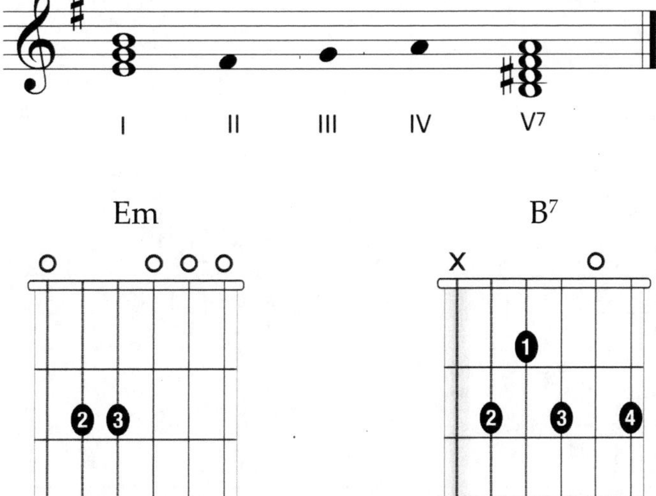

Practice strumming the E minor key progression:

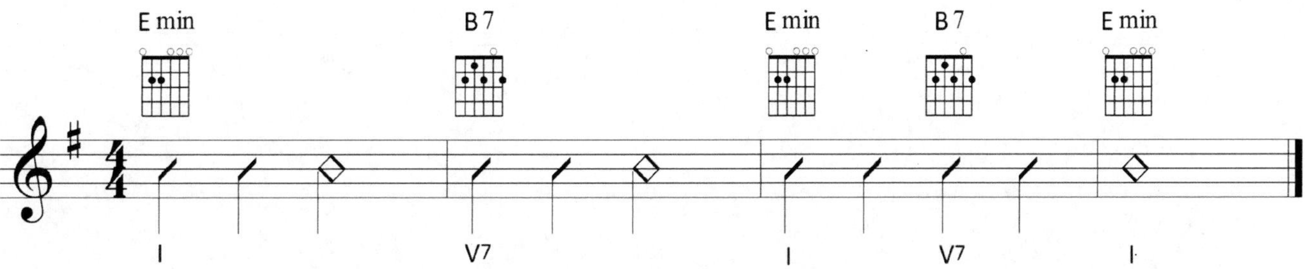

string are played free stroke. For example:

Invention in E Minor No. 1

AUDIO 13

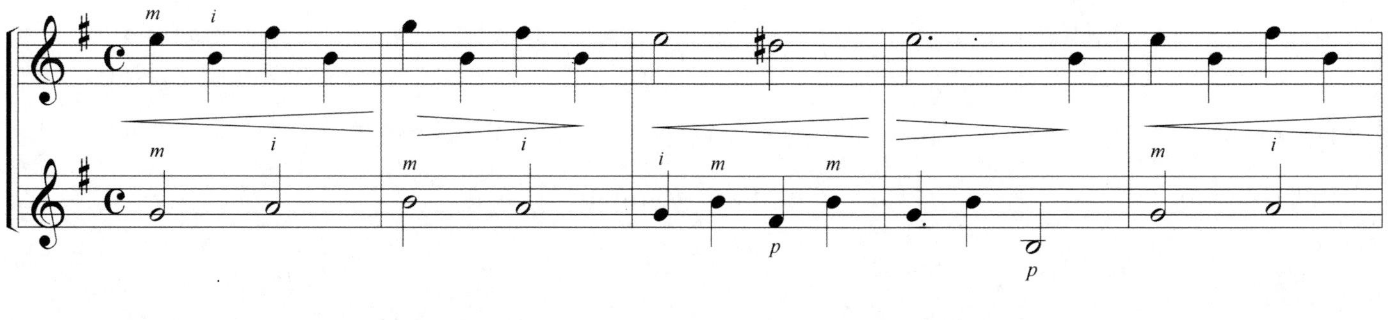

rit. . . p .
Harm XIII

Invention in E Minor No. 2

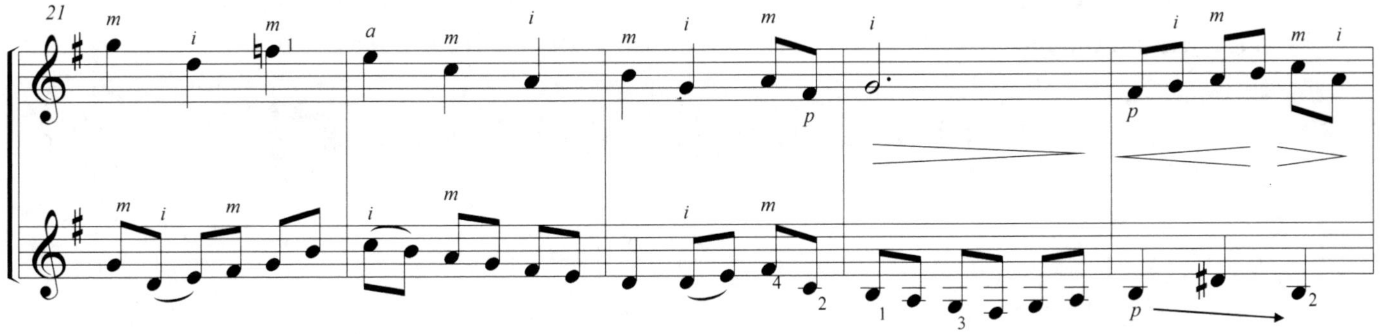

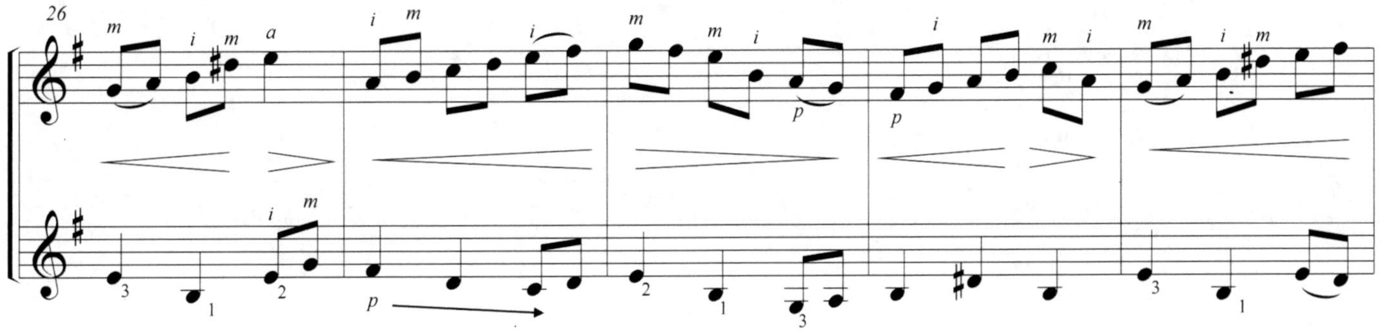

Invention in E Minor No. 3

Invention in E Minor No.3 includes a short-long rhythmic pattern in $\frac{6}{8}$. Before pre-reading, practice clapping and counting aloud the following excerpts until secure:

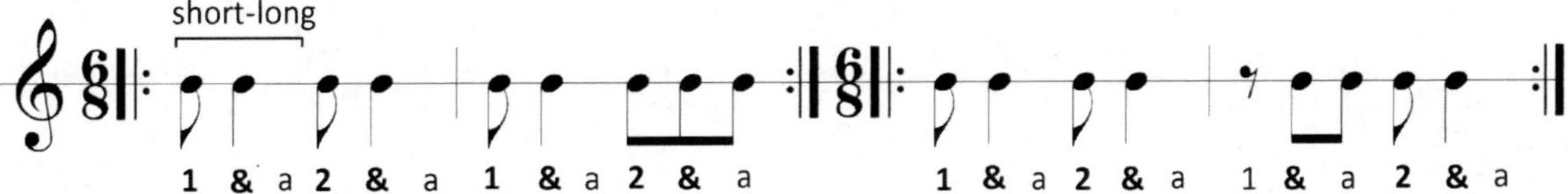

The Guitar II part in *Invention in E Minor No. 3* involves considerable alternation of *p* and fingers which should be played *free stroke*. Where alternation is primarily fingers, play *rest stroke*.

Invention in E Minor No. 3

27
(free)
32
simile
37
42
48
1.
2.
rit. . . . .

A (la) on ①

The highest sounding note found in this Book 1s A (la) on ① which is formed at **V**. In order to reach with "4," you'll need to shift your hand into second position.

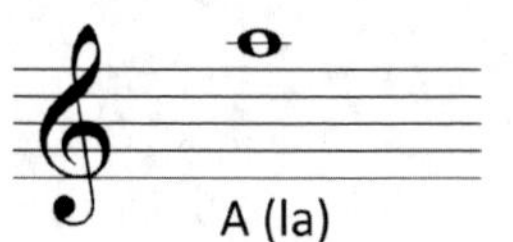

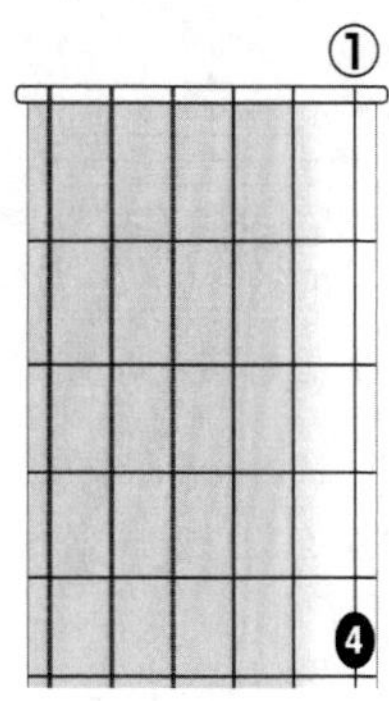

Be able to practice Ex. 17 while looking at the fingerboard.

Ex. 17

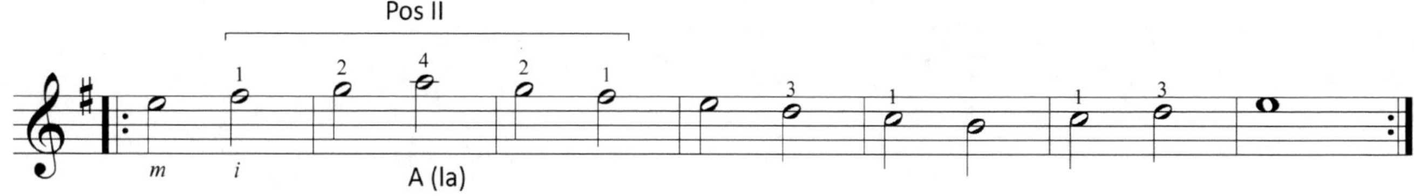

The following duet, *Andante* introduces A on ①. Play rest stroke throughout. Remember to carefully pre-read, if necessary one line at a time.

Andante

Two Slur Studies

The following solos, *Berry Pickin'* and *Balinese* are slur studies. Remember to articulate slurs rhythmically even with your left hand. Strive to sound the second slurred note in equal volume to the first.

In Berry Picking, notice the A (la) on ① starting at m. 9. In addition, notice the *D.S. al Coda (dal segno al coda)* marking at m. 34 which means to repeat back to the sign, 𝄌 , at m. 17, play through to the 𝄋 at m. 25 and then jump to the next 𝄌 at m. 35 to play the *coda* (ending).

EIGHTH- AND SIXTEENTH-NOTE PATTERNS

So far in this book you've played rhythms no quicker than an a eighth note. *Balinese* (p. 72) is the first to include sixteenth notes. While most sixteenth-note patterns should be familiar, a brief overview is helpful.[13] Recall that the typical manner of counting sixteenths is **1**-e-&-a, **2**-e-&-a , etc.

In *Balinese*, an eighth/sixteenth pattern is found and articulated with slurs:

To best develop rhythmic understanding and accuracy, you should begin by counting aloud and clapping the pattern without the slur:

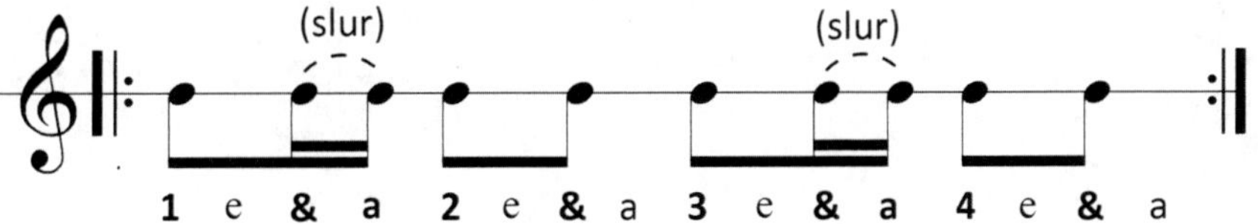

...next, practice playing in a simple context. Continue counting while you play, being sure to articulate the sixteenth notes evenly and accurately.

[13] For more information on 16th notes, see *Book 1*, p. 101.

Balinese

ALTERNATING REST STROKE *A* AND FREE STROKE *P-I-M*

One very beautiful technique of guitar playing involves alternating rest and free stroke. When properly executed, the qualities of the two different strokes produce a melody/accompaniment type of texture. Melody is played with rest stroke and accompaniment, with free stroke.

One of the easiest introductions to this technique involves *a* rest stroke, followed by free stroke on adjacent stings with fingers and *p*. Additional right-hand tilt toward the thumb will allow *a* to extend into its rest-stroke position while maintaining *p-i-m* free stroke. In the following examples, it's important to *release* the "resting" of *a* immediately after playing ① to make ② available for *m*. Notice rest stroke is indicated with "**v**" sign above the note.

Ex. 18a—Contrasting Rest and Free Stroke—Adjacent Strings

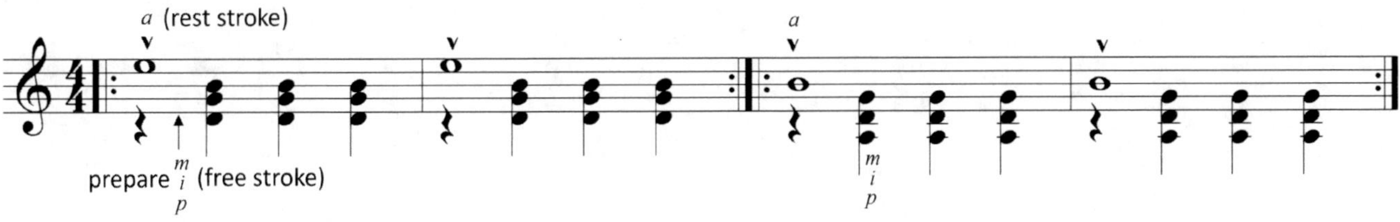

Ex. 18b—Contrasting Rest and Free Stroke—Non-Adjacent Strings

Ex. 18c—Alternating Rest and Free Stroke:

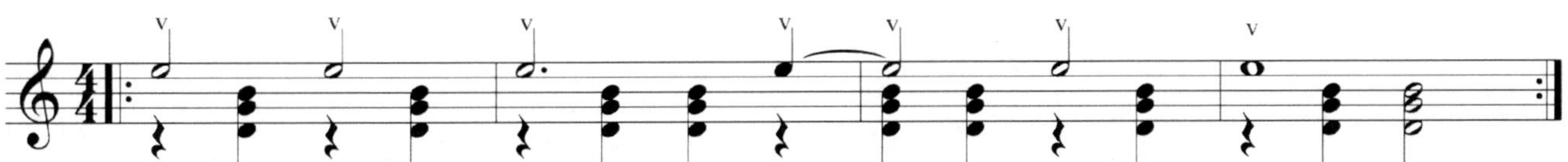

Ex. 18d—Alternating Rest and Free Stroke with String Crossing:

Lyric Tune I

C (do) on ③

C (do) on ③ at **V** is most readily reached with "4" with the left hand in Pos II. Be able to say and play the following while looking at the fingerboard:

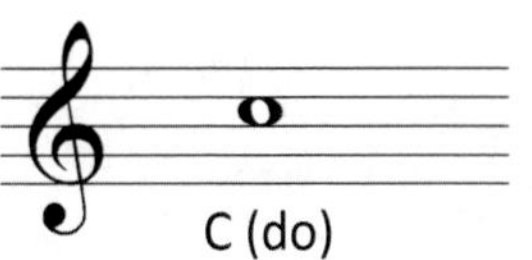

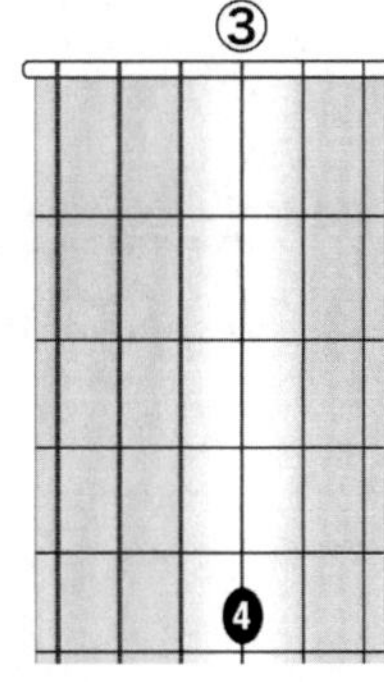

Ex. 19

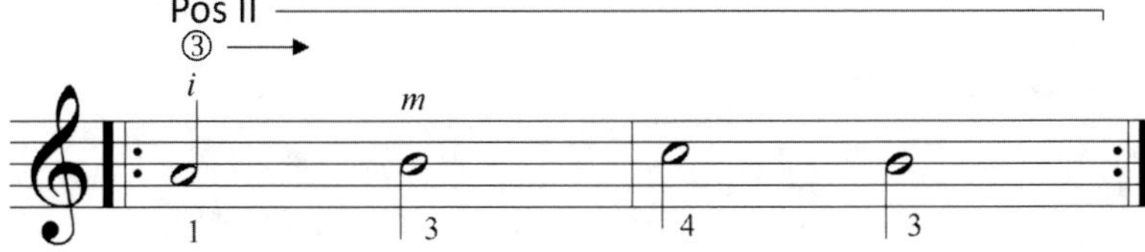

CAMPANELLA

With the addition of C on ③, it's now possible to consider an alternate way to realize scalar passages on adjacent strings. Consider the following:

Ex. 20

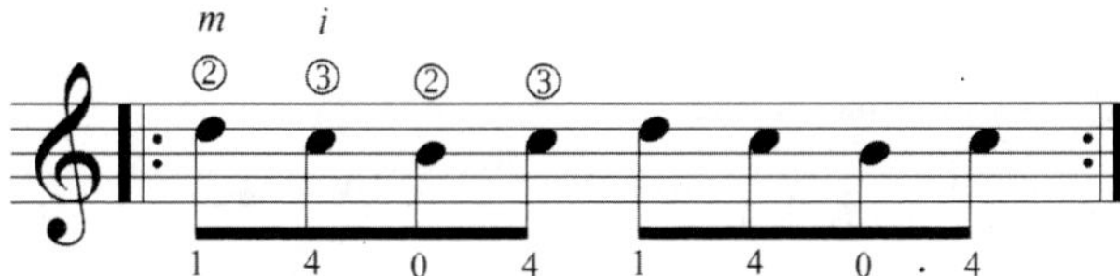

Notice that *higher* note C is on a *lower* string, and *lower* note B is on a *higher* string. When a scalar passage is organized as this, it's referred to as having *campanella* (bell-like) fingering with each note ringing over the next. With this as the goal, campanella passages should always be played *free stroke*. In the example above, notice the fingering for D—"1" on ②. This allows the left hand to more comfortably relax, while technically in third *position* (Pos III).

The following solo *Campanella*, applies this fingering. When pre-reading, be sure to carefully visualize, if necessary clarifying right- and left-hand requirements in small segments. For example:

The opening measure:

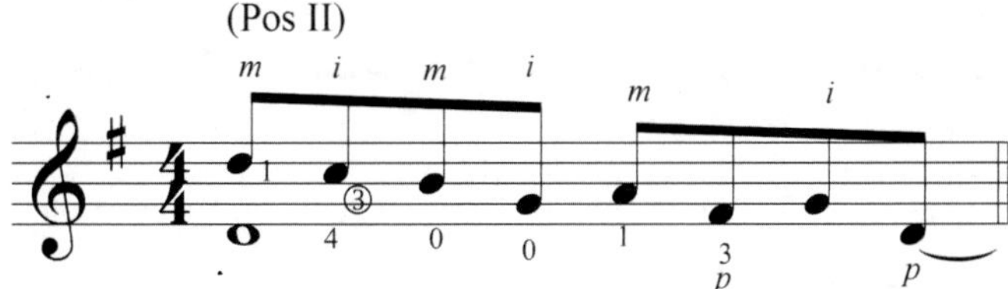

...realized for the right hand on open strings:

Campanella

(play free stroke throughout)

Dorian Tune

The following solo, *Dorian Tune,* makes use of a new chord played in the 3rd position, marked *Pos III.*

This is realized on the fingerboard as:

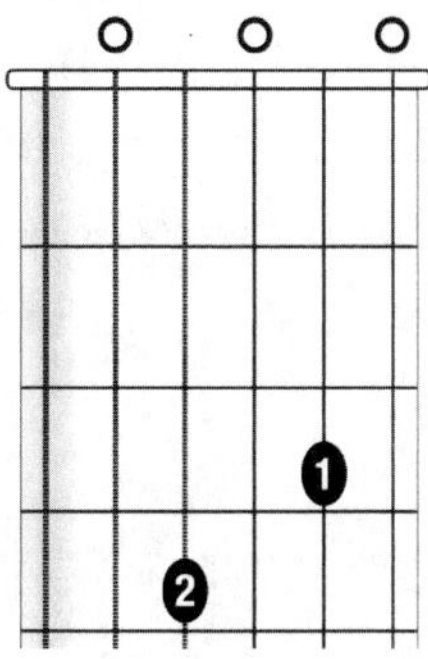

The following example is a simplification of the first four measures of *Dorian Tune*. Notice the left-hand pattern from chord to chord. The fingers simply glide shift along the same strings holding their shape from open position to Pos III and back.

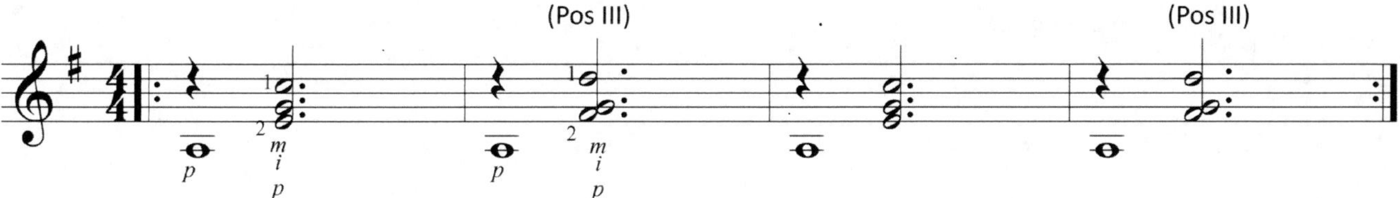

In mm. 4 & 12 of *Dorian Tune,* C on ③ is indicated as follows:

Isolating the stems-up-part, the campanella fingering becomes apparent with *high* note C on a *lower* string, and *lower* note B is on a *higher* string.

In the second half of the piece, notice *a* rest-stroke markings (mm. 21-32). Be sure to immediately release the resting *a* from its lower adjacent string, to allow *m* to sound its string.

TASTO

As you have already experienced in rest stroke, the tone, or *color*, of the guitar changes, depending how string are played. Another way of altering color has to do with *where* the string is played. If the right hand plays over the neck, indicated *tasto*, the sound becomes dark or mellow.[14] At the end of a *tasto* passage, the marking *ordinary* (abbreviated as *ord.*) indicates that the right hand returns to its normal position over the sound hole. Practice moving between *ord.* and *tasto*. When first learning this technique, you may need to stabilize your right hand by touching *m* on a treble string while playing and shifting.

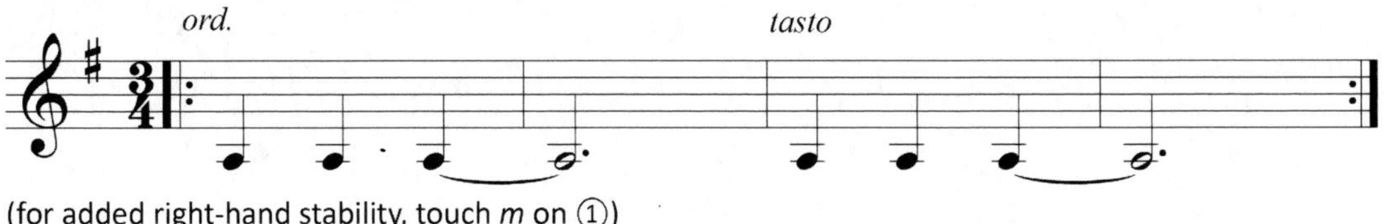

...next, practice gradually moving in and out of *tasto*:

Tasto occurs in *Dorian Tune* between mm. 16-28. In addition, notice the *D.C al Coda (da capo al coda)* marking at m. 32 which means to repeat back to the beginning, play through to the 𝄌 at m. 15 and then jump to 𝄌 at m. 33 to play the coda (ending).

[14] Also known as *sul tasto*.

Dorian Tune

tasto
(move to ord.)
ord.
tasto
(move to ord.)
ord.
rit.
D.C. al Coda
Harm. VII

PLAYING CHORDS *P-I-A*

Playing *p-i-a* chords is very similar to *p-i-m* chords. The main concern is to lift *m* slightly when flexing so as to not touch the strings. As when playing *p-i-m* chords, do not allow your hand to spring outward from the wrist.

As always, emphasize solid follow-through from the mid-joint and check that the basal joints do not flex too much (see the DVD).

Ex. 21

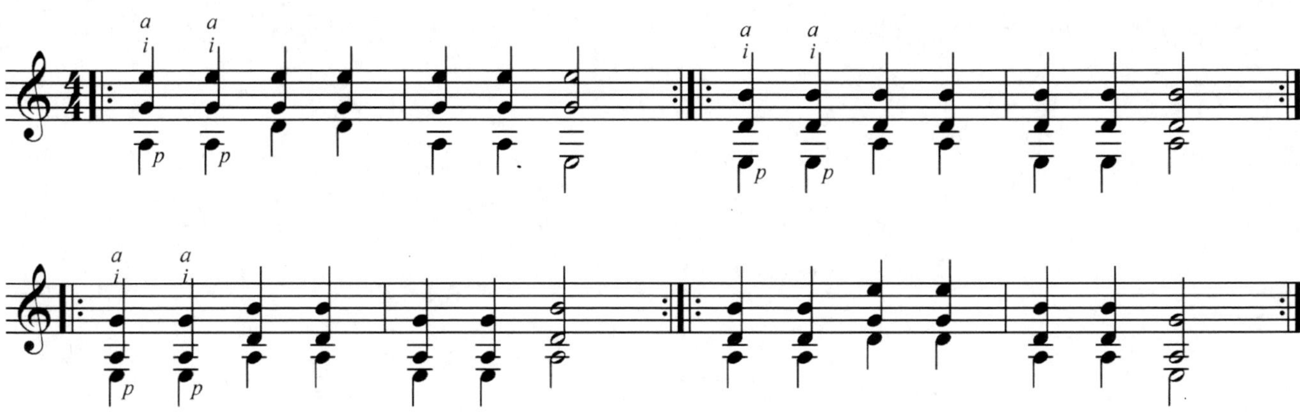

You'll find application of *p-i-a* beginning with *Chord study No. 5, Bells,* (p. 81).

PONTICELLO

Another type of tone color is *ponticello.*[15] Ponticello, (abbreviated as *pont.*) indicates that the right hand is repositioned to play below the sound hole, near the bridge. This temporarily changes the sound to a "brighter" tone quality. As with *tasto, ord* marks the end of a *ponticello* passage, indicating the right hand returns to its normal position over the sound hole. Practice changing from *ord.* to *pont.*:

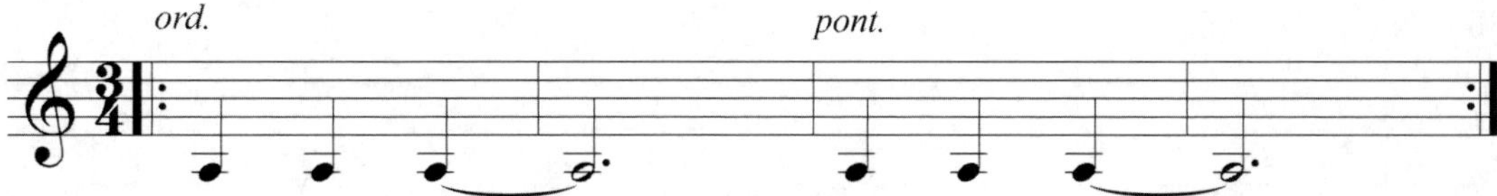

Next, apply ponticello to *p-i-a* chords.

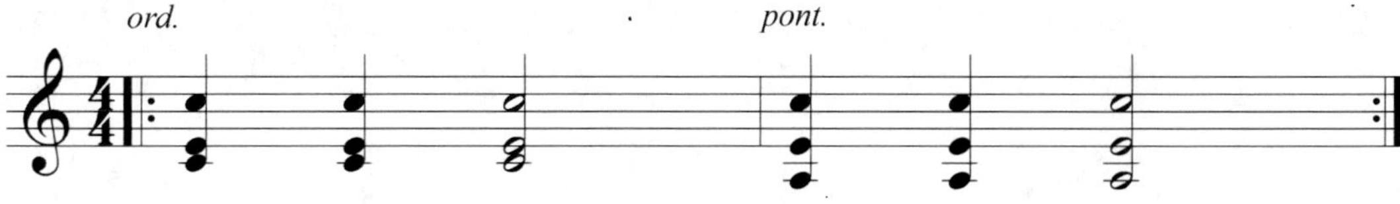

---

[15] Also known as *sul ponticello.*

Ponticello occurs in *Bells* at mm. 17-24. Be sure to carefully pre-read, one phrase or line at a time.

Bells

Chord Study No. 5

WWW The following studies include a mixture of *p-i-a* and *p-i-m* chords.

Andante Grazioso

AUDIO 17

Chord Study No. 6

W.A. Mozart

STACCATO

The following chord study, *Chorale St. Antoni* makes use of a *staccato* articulation, indicated by a dot above a chord.

Staccato means to shorten the rhythmic duration of a note or chord. This is easily realized on the guitar by playing and then immediately returning your fingers to the strings in the manner of a prepared stroke.

Practice Staccato in the following:

WWW

Chorale St. Antoni

Chord Study No. 7

Greensleeves

Chord Study No. 8

rit.

a tempo

f p strum

f p strum

rit. . . . .

The Key of D Major

Establishing tonic D (re) and *leading tone* to C♯ (di) creates the key of *D major*. In order to conform to the whole/half step pattern, the key signature now includes two sharps.

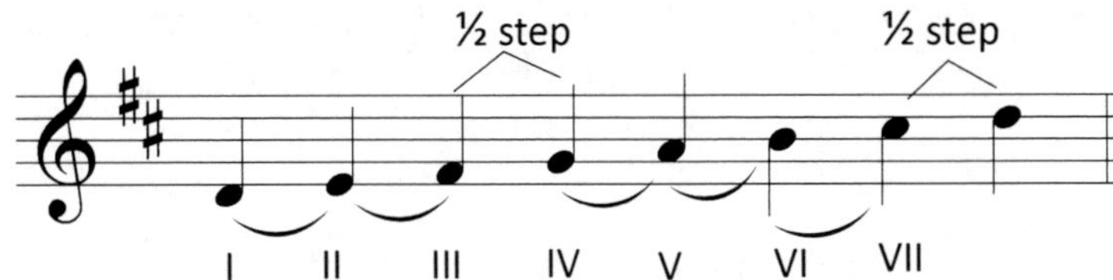

Review all open-position notes in the key D major. Notice the new note A (la) as the upper limit of pitch range.

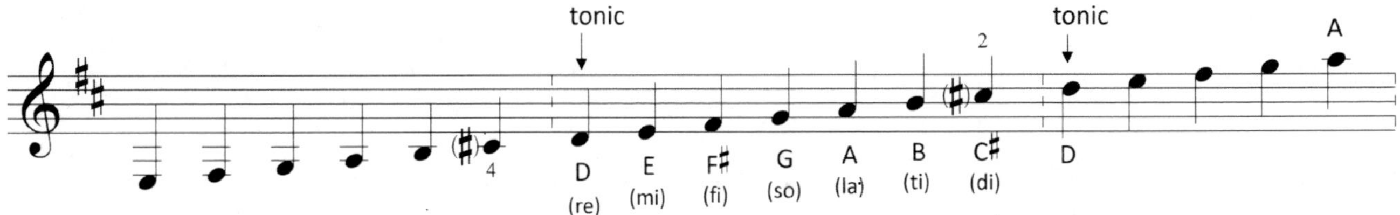

The D-major scale is unique in that none of fret I notes are needed. Thus, the scale is easily played with the left hand in Pos II (with "1" oriented above fret II), allowing you to reach A on ①. Pre-read, practice, and memorize the following D-major scale. Practice first with *free* and then with *rest stroke*.

- Vocalize note names and locate/touch all the leading-tone C♯ (di)'s.
- Begin slowly at first; when you can play the scale securely, accelerate the tempo, but continue to play without hesitation.
- When secure, be able to play one stroke-per-note from memory.

Harmony

In the key of D major, the **I** chord is D and the **V**^{7} chord is A^7.

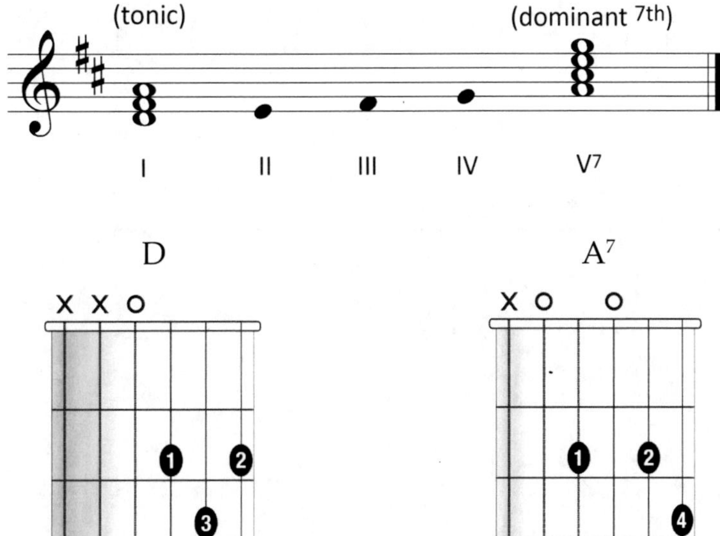

Practice strumming the key progression:

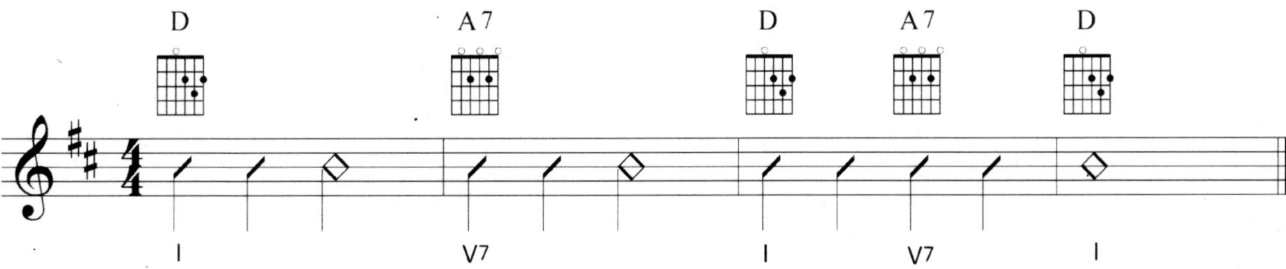

Invention in D Major No. 1

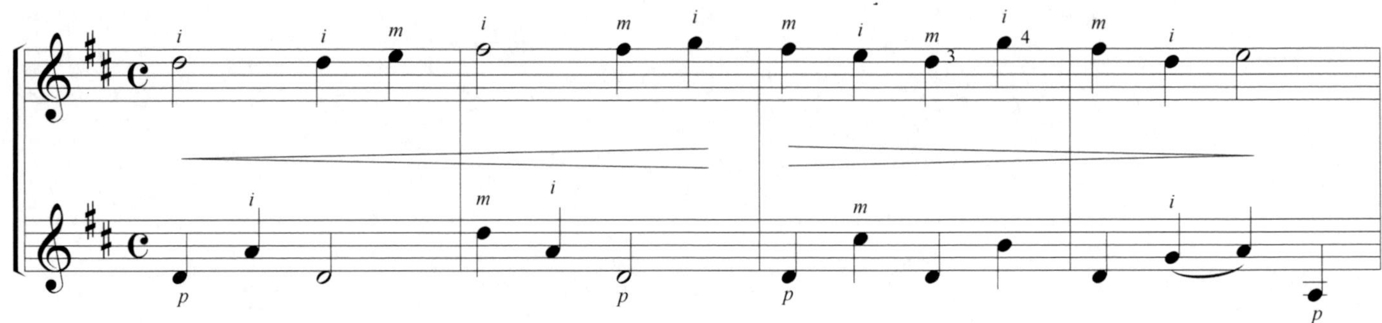

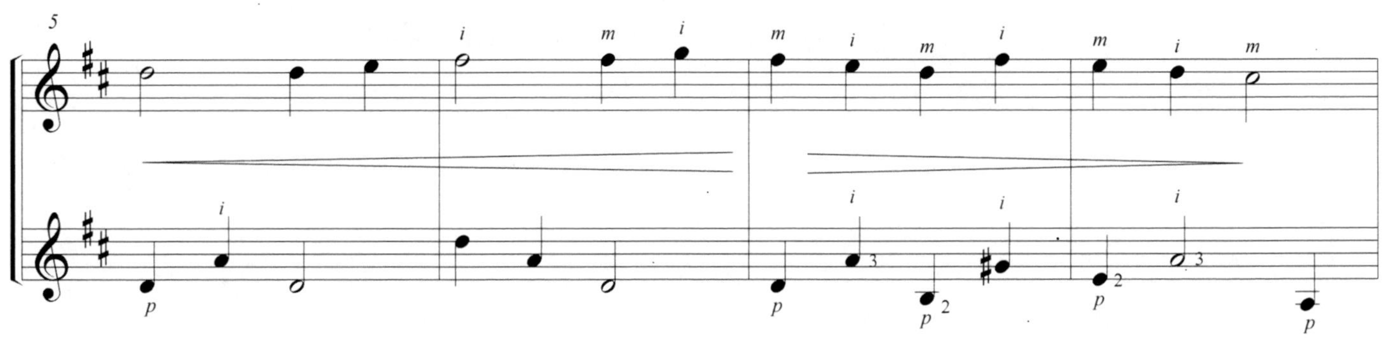

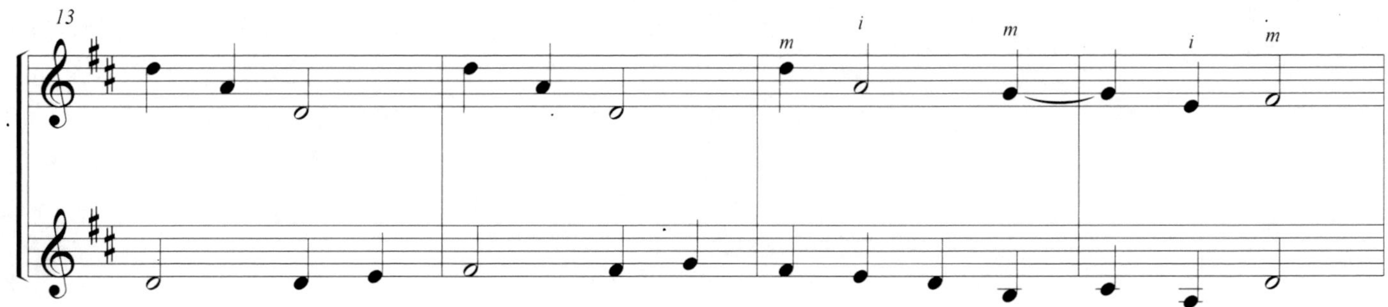

17

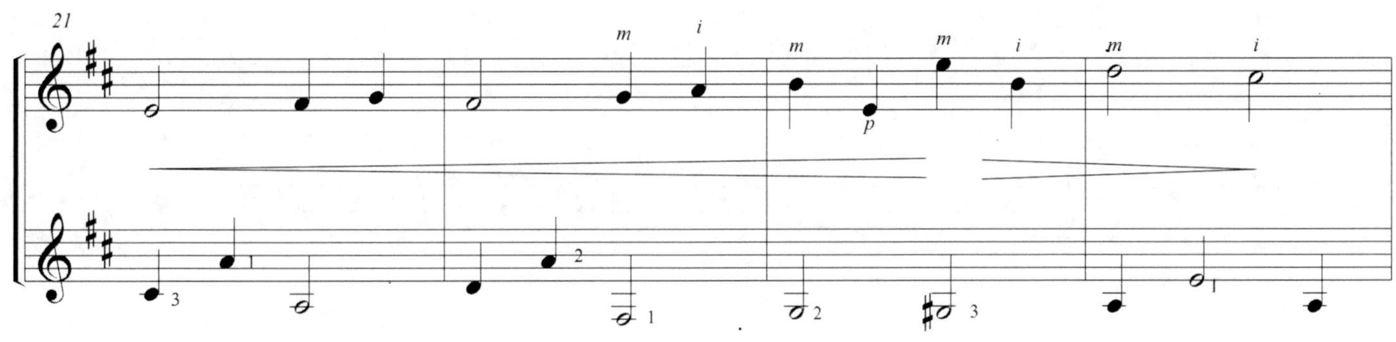
21

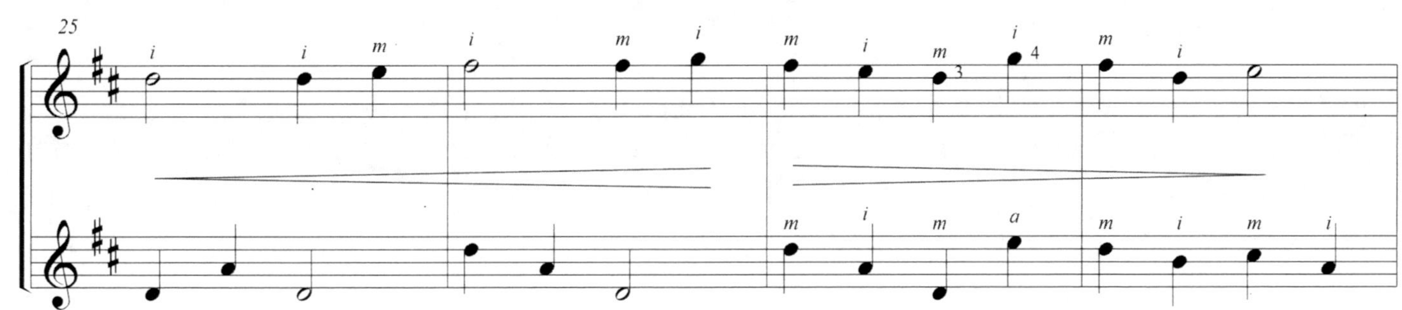
25

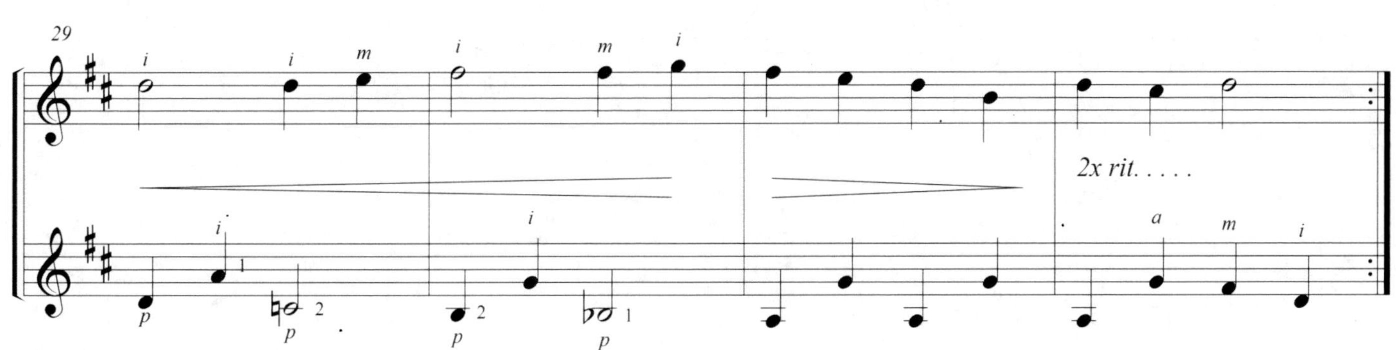
29
2x rit. . . . .

Invention in D Major No. 2

AUDIO 20

Invention in D Major No. 3

Two simultaneous syncopated rhythms occur in *Invention in D Major No. 3*. Count aloud and clap each part:

Guitar I part syncopation:

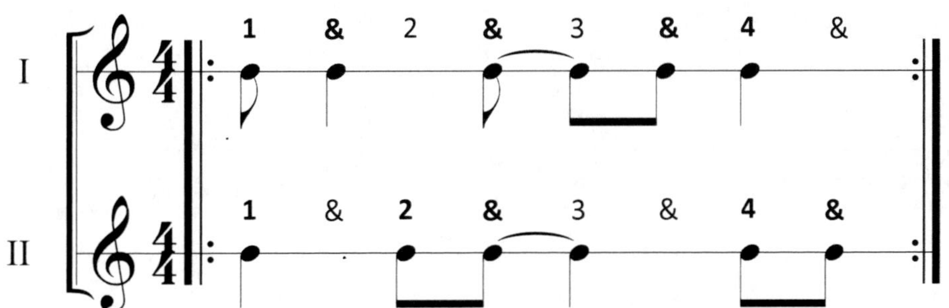

Guitar II part syncopation:

Invention in D Major No. 3

AUDIO 21

BARRING

Barring refers to pressing two or more strings simultaneously against a single fret with the first finger of the L.H. The notation for barring in this method is the letter "B." If necessary, other symbols such as the Roman numeral to indicate fret number, and a small circled number to indicate the strings to be barred may be included. For example:

- BII③ indicates a bar across three strings at the second fret.
- BI⑥ indicates a full bar (across all six strings) at the first fret.

A bracket extending from the "B," shows how long to hold the bar. Following are examples of barring notation:

Ex. 22

When barring, you must learn to allow the first finger to flatten, creating a reasonably even surface with which to create the bar. In cases where other fingers are placed on the fingerboard in addition to the bar, the first finger may sometimes rotate slightly to the left. Be sure to study the DVD carefully to form a clear understanding of this technique.

You will begin barring the first three strings at the second fret, which is easier than barring all six strings. As you practice Ex. 23, focus on developing control of the tip joint of the first finger.

Ex. 23

It is important to remember that developing the ability to bar will require strengthening of the hand, so be sure to work patiently, and to stop and rest whenever you begin to feel discomfort. This skill must be developed gradually to avoid pain and potential injury (see Repetitive Strain Injury on line).

A Temporary Notation for Reading Barred Chords

The following study, *Bar Blues*, provides practice with simple bars on three adjacent strings. To make reading easier, a temporary notation has been devised for this piece *only*. This special notation makes the following considerations:

- each chord will involve *only* L.H. finger "1."
- each chord will contain *only* notes formed at the indicated fret on three adjacent strings.
- the highest note of the chord is notated, but lower notes are indicated with a rectangular box.
- *"B" + a Roman Numeral* indicates which fret to bar.
- circled numbers indicate which strings to be played.

Thus instead of reading this:

........you'll read only an F♯ with a lower rectangular extension:

Consider the first two measures of *Bar Blues*. If written in standard notation, it would appear as:

... with special barring notation the same passage will read:

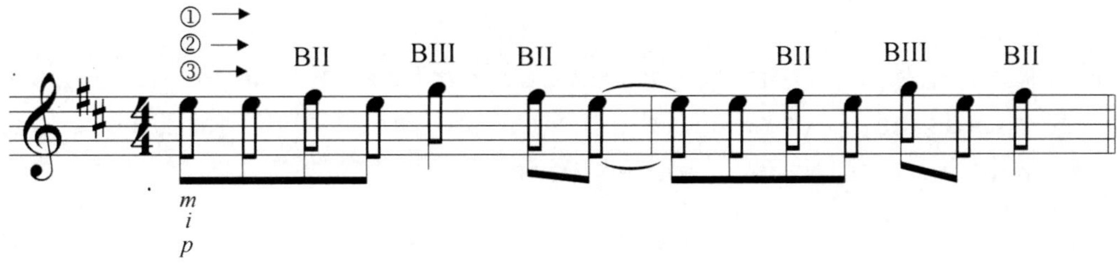

Remember, *"B" + a Roman numeral*, indicates which fret to bar; if no "B" is shown, the chord is understood as open strings.

Bar Blues

IMPORTANT: From this point forward, this special *Bar Blues* notation is no longer used. While reading barred chords may present a challenge, the indication of "B"(and a bracket) will aid in the quick visualization of notes on the other strings.

The Key of B Minor

The relative of D major is B minor with a key signature of two sharps and tonic B. Below is the scale's whole-/half-step pattern which is characteristic of natural minor.

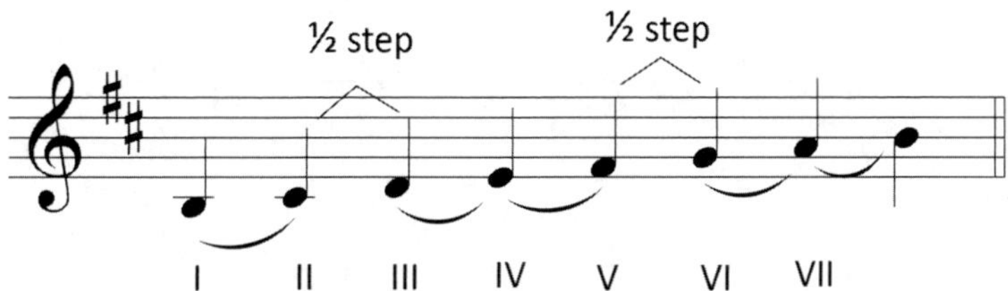

B Natural Minor Scale

Review all of the open-position notes in B natural minor. A on ① is shown in parenthesis, meaning that while not included in the scales, will be found in the music of this section.

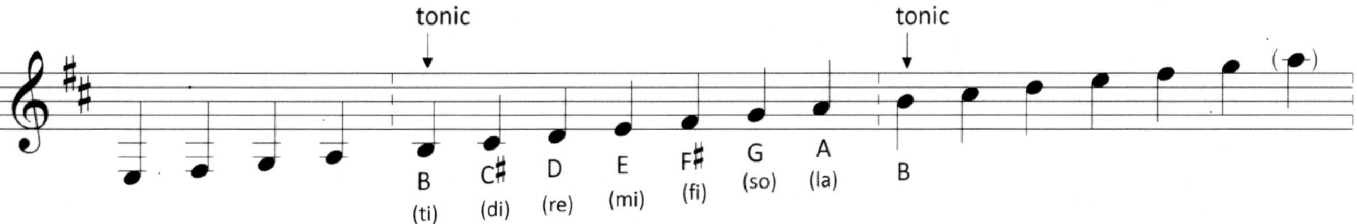

B Harmonic Minor

Adding the accidental A♯ (li) to B natural minor creates a leading tone and changes the mode to *harmonic minor*.

Pre-read, practice, and memorize the following *B harmonic minor* scale.

B Melodic Minor

Adding accidentals G♯ (si) and A♯ (li) raises degrees **VI** and **VII**, changing the scale to B *melodic minor.*

Pre-read, practice, and memorize the following *B melodic minor* scale.

Be able to play both harmonic and melodic minor scales, one stroke-per-note from memory.

Harmony

In the key of B minor, the tonic **I** is Bm and the dominant **V**^{7} is F♯^{7}.

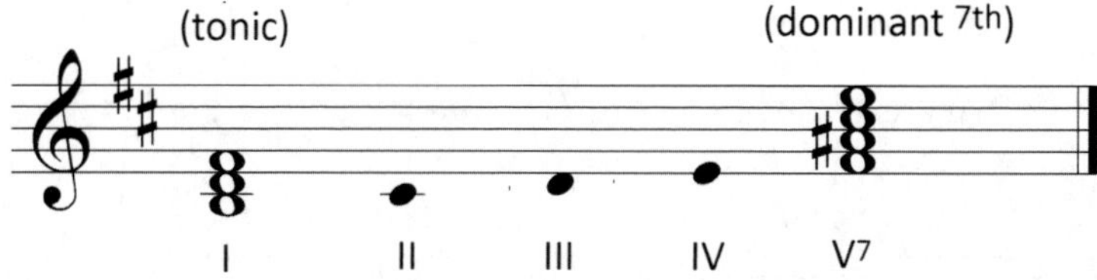

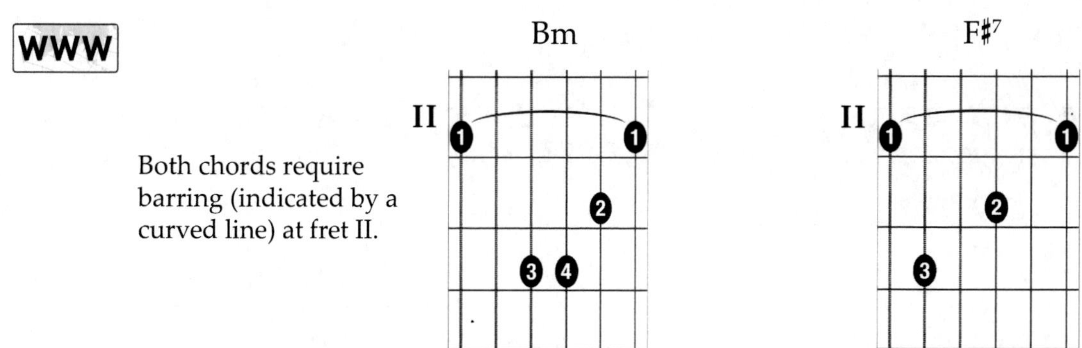

Both chords require barring (indicated by a curved line) at fret II.

Practice strumming the key progression of B minor.

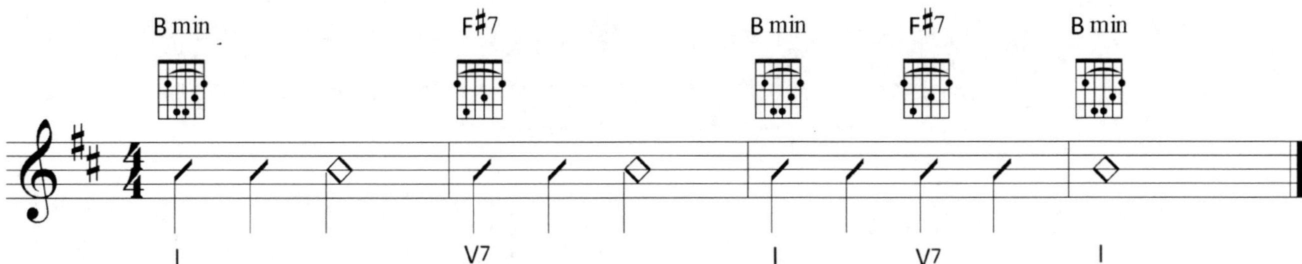

New Rhythms

A new pattern—the dotted eighth/sixteenth, is introduced in *Invention in B Minor No. 3* (p. 104). A dot next to an eighth means it receives the first three sixteenth counts (1 e & a)

The rhythm of the first 4 measures of the Guitar I part is shown below. Practice counting aloud and clapping.

HEMIOLA

Invention in B Minor No.1 features a *hemiola* (pron. hee-mee-*oh*-la) rhythm, a shift in beat grouping, most often between two and three. For example in music written in $\frac{3}{4}$, there are a total of 6 eighth notes in each measure. These notes can be organized either as three groups of 2, or two groups of 3.

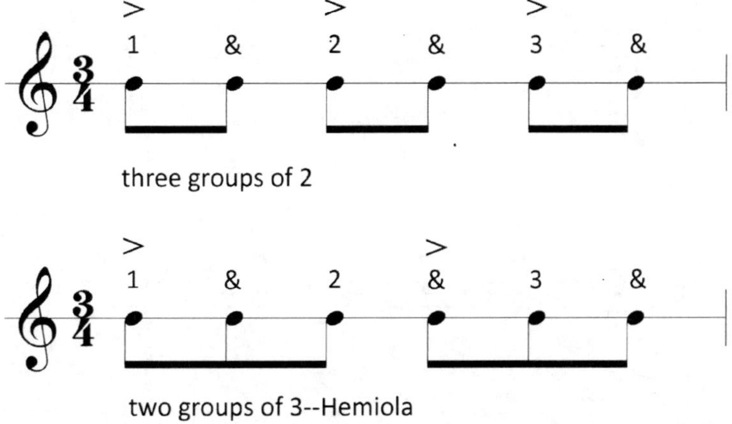

The later grouping in $\frac{3}{4}$ is the hemiola. The same situation, though reversed, can be found in $\frac{6}{8}$ meter.

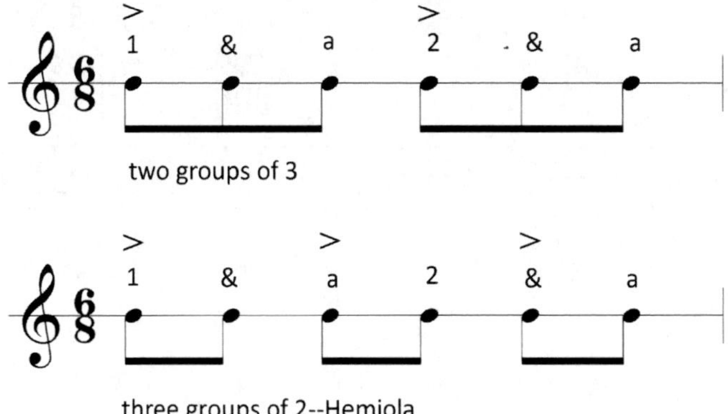

Invention in B Minor No.1 is written in $\frac{3}{4}$ with hemiola occurring in the lower part.

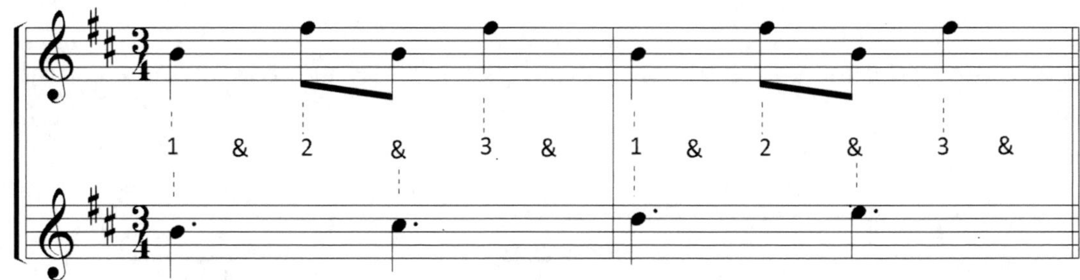

For the most sonorous effect, play passages with alternating adjacent strings with free stroke as indicated.

Invention in B Minor No. 1

(free stroke)
(rest stroke)
B
Harm VII

Invention in B Minor No. 2

17
21
25
29
33

In your pre-read, be sure to clarify the new 16th note rhythms by clapping and counting aloud.

Invention in B Minor No. 3

AUDIO 24

21
24
rit. . . . .
a tempo
27
31
34
1.
2.
rit. . . . .

REST STROKE FINGERS AND FREE STROKE ARPEGGIO

So far you've alternated rest-stroke fingers with free-stroke chords. Now you'll begin alternating a rest-stroke finger with a free-stroke arpeggio. As before, the combination of rest and free strokes is well suited for playing melody and accompaniment, where the melody is *rest*, and the accompaniment, *free*. For example, consider the following melody:

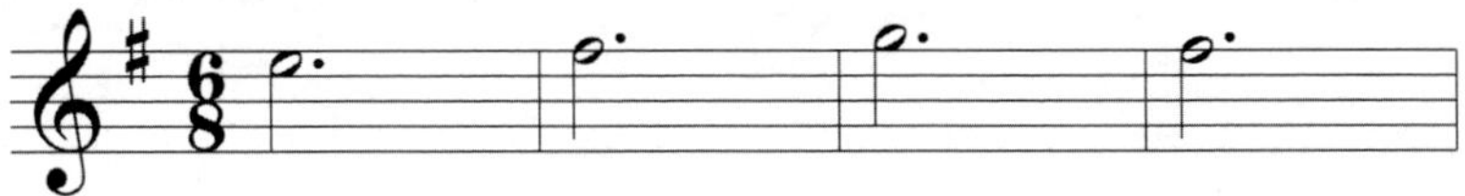

...the same melody with an arpeggiated accompaniment underneath:

The following solo *Lyric Tune II* makes use of this technique. Begin by practicing on open strings and consider the following:

- Your right-hand position is in optimal position with *a* slightly more extended than other fingers.
- Be sure to immediately release resting *a*, allowing your other fingers to move freely on lower adjacent strings.
- Remember that "**v**" indicates rest stroke.

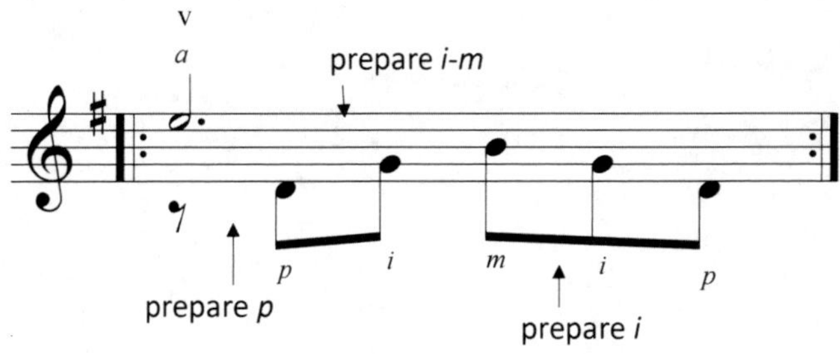

D (re) on ⑤

At m. 22 of *Lyric Tune II* there is a D (re) on ⑤, played at fret V with "3". This requires a momentary shift into Pos III. Carefully visualize this movement during your pre-reading.

THIS PAGE LEFT INTENTIONALLY BLANK

Lyric Tune II

rit.......
a tempo
rit.......
a tempo
1.
2.
rit. . . .

ALTERNATING REST-STROKE FINGERS AND *P* FREE STROKE

Alternating rest and free strokes in close juxtaposition occurs in passages where both melody and bass lines are rhythmically active. The next solo, *Lyric Tune III* addresses that challenge with a right-hand pattern similar to what is shown in Ex. 24a. Consider the following before practicing:

- Place your hand is in its optimal position.
- If support for *p* free stroke is needed, each rest-stroked finger may remain resting on its lower adjacent string until the next melody note is stroked.
- For best continuity, release the resting finger from its lower adjacent string immediately after stroking.
- Practice the following from memory, watching the right hand.

Ex. 24a

Ex. 24b provides further practice with rest fingers and *p* free in steady alternation:

Ex. 24b

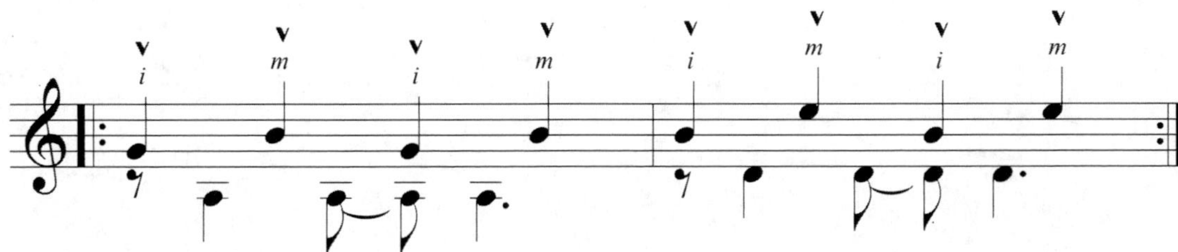

Lyric Tune III

As with the other Lyric Tunes, rest stroke is indicated with a "**v**" When the symbol is not present, the passage is assumed to be played free as seen in mm. 8-9:

Lyric Tune III

CHORDS OF FOUR NOTES

In sounding chords of four notes (*p-i-m-a*), you should concentrate on the firm placement and flexion of *a*. Give special attention to bringing out the highest note of each chord, which in the example below is also the melody. Aim for an even execution and a feeling of security as you change from one chord to the next.

Ex. 25

CHORD VISUALIZATION

Giving attention to the *a* finger to bring out the melody in pima chords is also important for visualizing chords. The melody note, often the highest sounding note in a chordal structure serves as a syllabic cue that evokes a larger movement form—in this case, 4-note chords. Consider the folowing first four measures from *Chord Study No. 10*:

To visualize, scan the passage and carry out the following:

- Identify, if possible, the name of each chord. Chords are like words; naming them, identifies all of its parts, creates a visual pattern, and on a deeper level, provides contextual meaning. For example, you may recognize a chord as a C major. Mentally labeling it as such, forms an image of *one* complete idea, rather than *four* separate unrelated pitches. In addition, how does C major relate to the key of the piece; is it a **I**, a **IV**, or a **V**^{7} chord? Knowing something about it's harmonic function can add another label to the chord as well as provide an expection for memorization (for example,**V** frequently moves to **I**).

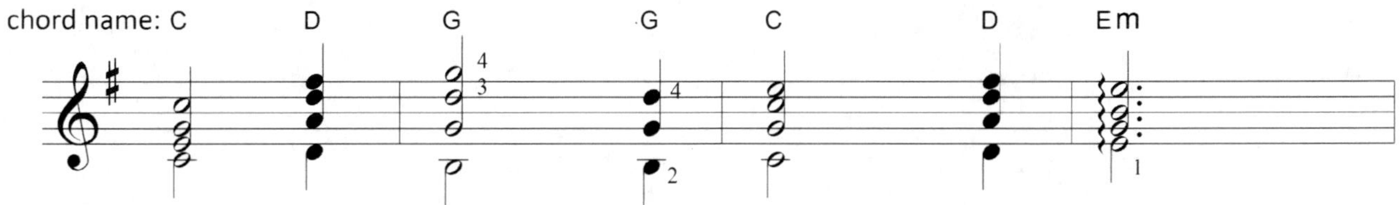

- Determine the left-hand connections. Often there are common tones from one chord to the next and that can benefit the player with a common fingering. If there are no left-hand connections, follow any fingering cues and/or *isolate* the movement, working out specific coordination to smoothly move from one shape to the next.[16]

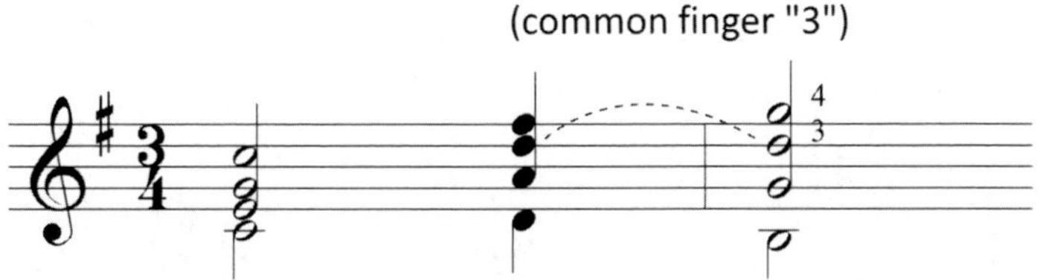

- When you've developed the movment vocabulary to securely articulate a segment or phrase, air-guitar it, vocalizing the melody note. Each melody note serves as syllabic cue to its connected chord:

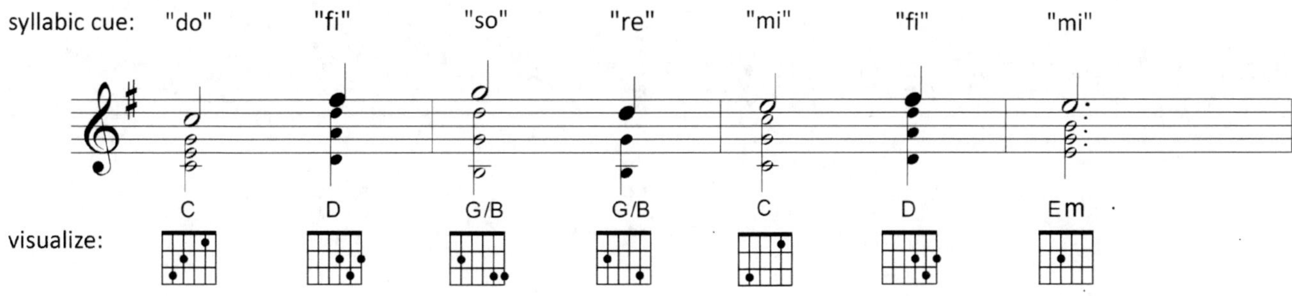

Chords in the following solo, *Eine Kleine Jazzmusik* are easy to form and their common tone/fingerings make them easy to connect from one to another. Be sure to follow fingerings. As jazz chords, however, they are a slightly difficult to label. Save this step for when visualizing all other chord studies.

[16] For information on isolations, see *Book 1*, p. 37.

WWW

Eine Kleine Jazzmusik I

Chord Study No. 9

THIS PAGE LEFT INTENTIONALLY BLANK

WWW

O Merciful Redeemer

AUDIO 25

Chord Study No. 10

Gustav Holst

rit..

WWW Notice the ponticello—mm. 25-26 and mm. 43-44.

El Noi de la Mare

AUDIO 26

Chord Study No. 11

f
pont.
D.C. al Coda
rit.
Harm VII

Barring with added left-hand fingers

The following studies, *Serenity* and *Bar Waltz*, involve barring with the added reach of L.H. fingers "2" and "4" (see video 32). Practice maintaining the bar on strings ①②③ while adding these fingers in the following exercises:

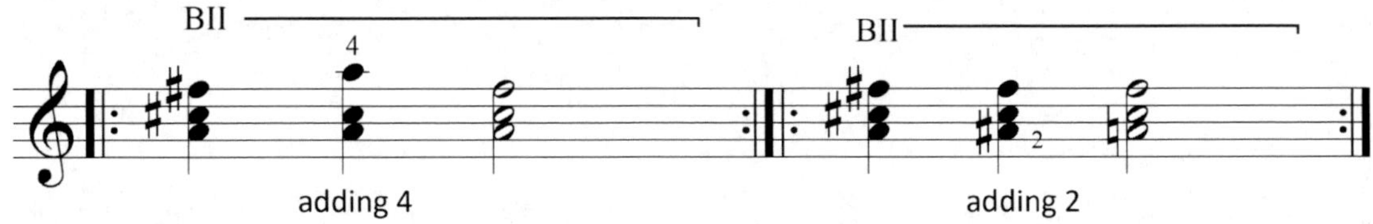

Both studies will be played predominantly in the second position. In *Serenity*, notice the ponticello at mm. 20-23.

Serenity

Moderately slow

16
BII
BII
19
rit.
a tempo
pont.
mp
22
ord.
BII
mf
25
BII
BII
BII
28
BII
BII
BII⑥
31
BII④
1.
BII⑥
34
2.
rit.
Harm VII

Bar Waltz

ARPEGGIOS WITHOUT *P*

The reference "without *p*" refers to an arpeggio where finger preparation is not preceded or "triggered" by a *p* free stroke. The simplest of these occurs when fingers play alone; but may also include arpeggios where *p* plays simultaneously with the arpeggio. The main point is that *p* alone does not initiate the pattern.

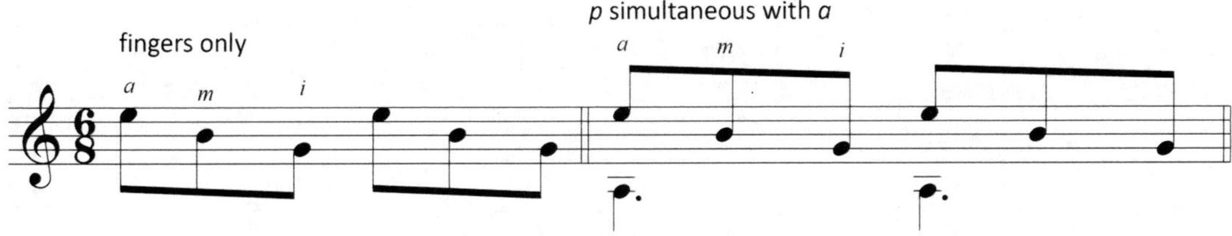

The first of the five arpeggios without *p* is *a, m, i*. You'll begin with sounding ①, ②, ③. Proceed as follows:

- Prepare *a-m* on ① and ②. Place *i* in a slightly flexed position.
- Flex *a* to sound ①.
- Flex *m* sympathetically with *a* to sound ②; as *m* flexes, simultaneously prepare *i* on ③.
- Flex *i* to sound ③; as *i* flexes, prepare *a-m* on ① and ②.
- As you do this, be sure to firmly flex *a* from the mid-joint to accent ①.

This arpeggio contains one sympathetic movement and one alternation: a sympathetic movement between *a* and *m*, followed by an alternation between *i* and *m-a*. Clearly understanding this relationship is one of the keys to avoiding excess tension during this arpeggio.

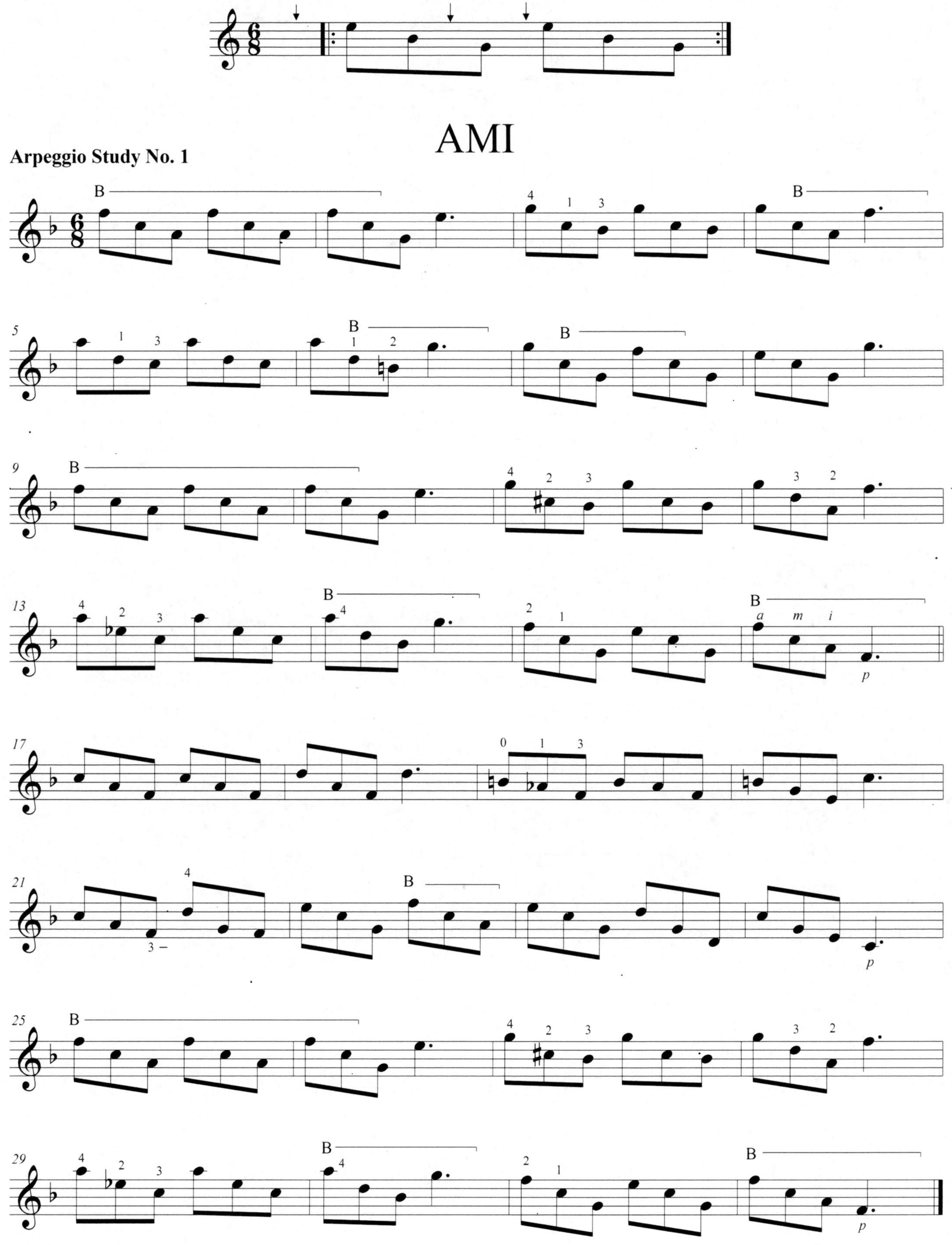

RHYTHM DANCE I - SYNCOPATION AND HEMIOLA

There are six solo etudes in the book entitled *Rhythm Dance* designed to further develop your skill with meter and rhythm. *Rhythm Dance I* is written in $\frac{3}{4}$ and features two rhythmic techniques—*syncopation* and *hemiola.* To aid your pre-reading, the following passages have been re-notated on open strings, allowing you to better visualize and coordinate the right-hand requirements.

Practice each, first clapping and counting aloud, then play slowly and count aloud until secure.

Ex. 26a—mm. 1-2 (syncopation)

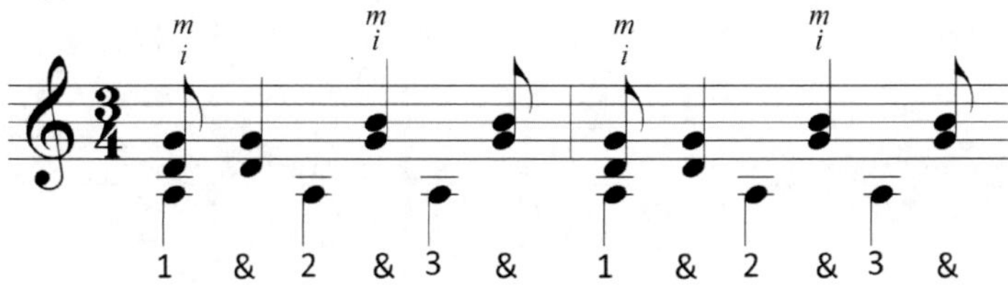

Ex. 26b—mm. 7-8 (syncopation and hemiola)

The *a,m,i* arpeggio without *p* is found throughout *Rhythm Dance I* in contexts with string crossing. These passages should be first practiced on open strings as seen in Exs. 26c and 26d. Be sure you're secure with the *a,m,i* form before proceeding.

Ex. 26c—mm. 15-16 (hemiola)

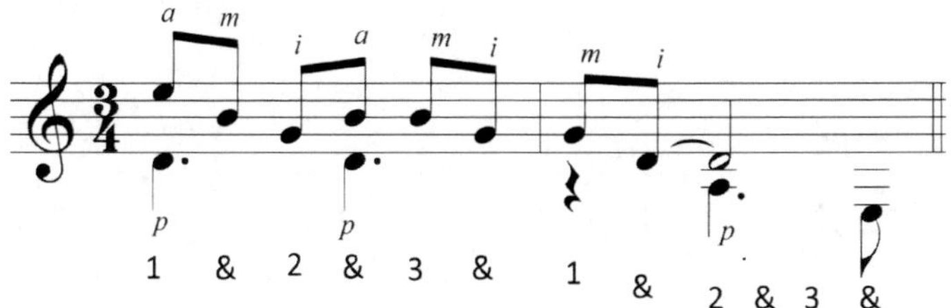

Ex. 26d—mm. 43-46 (hemiola)

Rhythm Dance I

25
m
i
a
28
m
i
f
rit. . . . . . .
a tempo
31
34
37
40
43
45
p
1.
2.

The Key of F Major

A tonic of F (fa) and all natural notes except B♭ (te) create the whole/half step pattern for *F major*. Observe the new key signature of one flat (B♭).

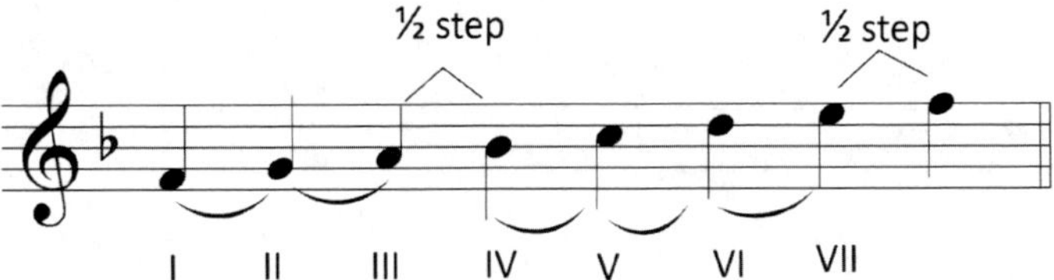

Review all open-position notes in the key F major. The A (la) on ① will not be incorporated into the scale but will be found in music of this section.

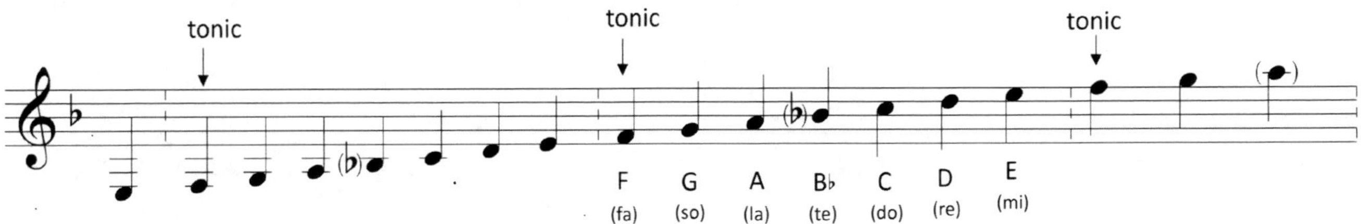

Pre-read, practice, and memorize the following F-major scale. Practice first with *free* and then with *rest stroke*.

- Learn to vocalize the notes of the scale and locate and touch all B♭ (te)'s.
- Begin slowly at first; when you can play the scale securely, accelerate the tempo, but continue to play without hesitation.
- When secure, be able to play one stroke-per-note from memory.

Harmony

In the key of F major, **I** is F and **V**[7] is C[7]. Notice that the F chord requires a bar at fret **I.**

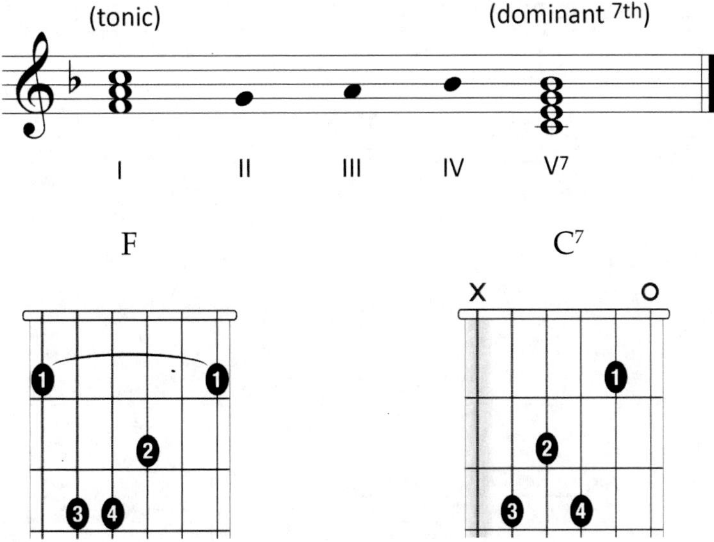

Practice strumming the key progression. When moving between the two chords, keep the common finger 3 on C (do).

Invention in F Major No. 1

Both parts in *Invention in F Major No. 1* should be played free stroke throughout. Music is written with a series of alternating melodic dyads that ring freely and harmonize between parts. The result is a two-part campanella texture.

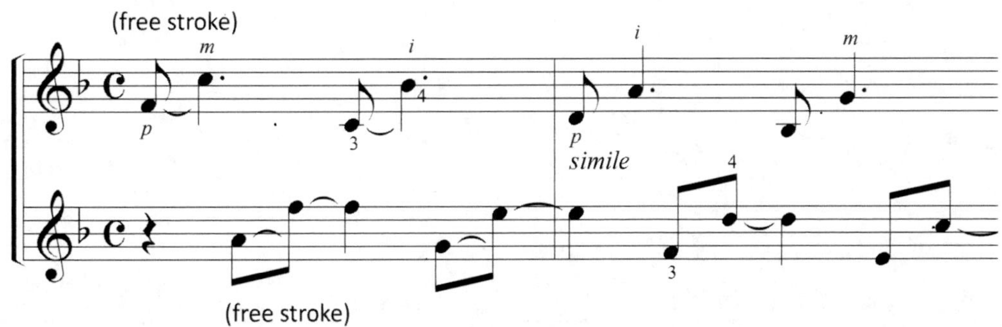

Invention in F Major No. 1

AUDIO 27

B
rit. . . . .
a tempo
1.
2.
rit. . . . .

Invention in F Major No. 2

AUDIO 28

BI
rit. . . . .
a tempo
1.
2.
rit. . . . .

COUNTING COMPOUND METER WITH 16TH NOTES

So far you've counted $\frac{6}{8}$ as 1, &, a, 2, &, a where the smallest rhythmic value is the eighth note. Sometimes in compound meter the smallest rhythmic unit is the 16th note, in which case new counting syllables are added in between. This is illustrated below:

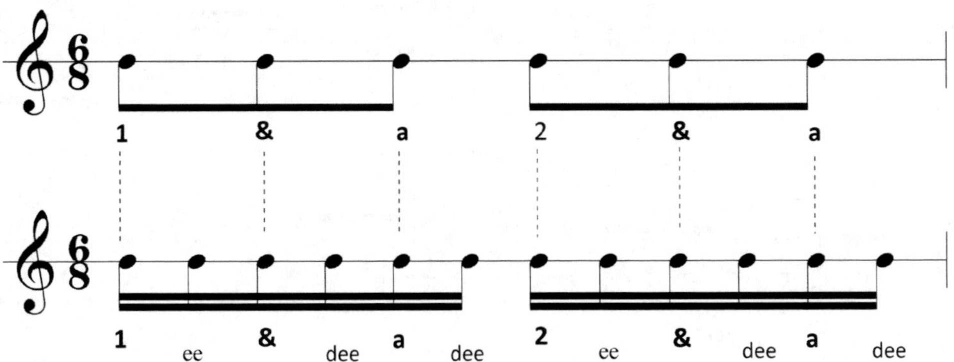

To allow the sixteenth counts to roll off your tongue, pronounce as:

"1-ee" "an-dee" "ah-dee" "2-ee" "an-dee" "ah-dee"

There are a variety of sixteenth-note rhythmic patterns in compound meter. Some of the more typical are shown below. Practice each counting aloud and clapping until secure.

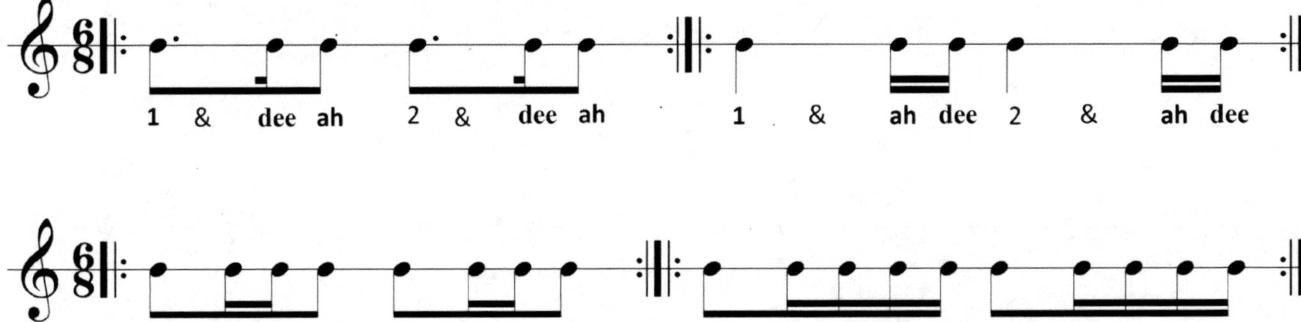

Invention in F major No. 3

Invention in F Major No. 3 is written in $\frac{6}{8}$ and uses several 16th-note patterns. Practice each, counting aloud and clapping until secure

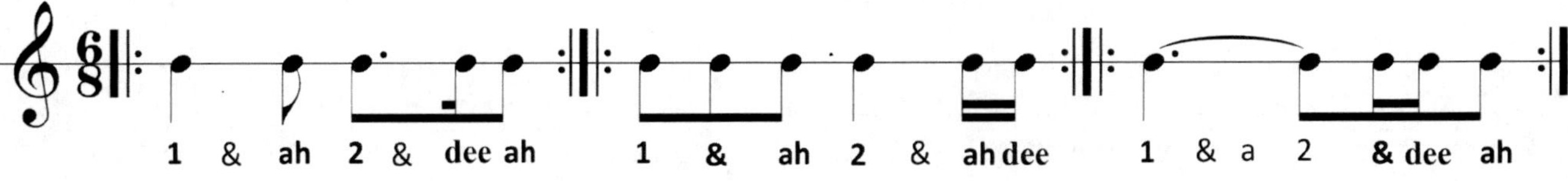

When pre-reading, notice the indefinite ties at m. 1.[17] This means you are to hold the notes as long as possible, allowing each to bleed over one another. The *simile* in the following measure indicates that you are to continue playing in this manner as long as possible.

Also notice the *hemiola* at m. 15 in the Guitar I part. In $\frac{6}{8}$ this should be counted:

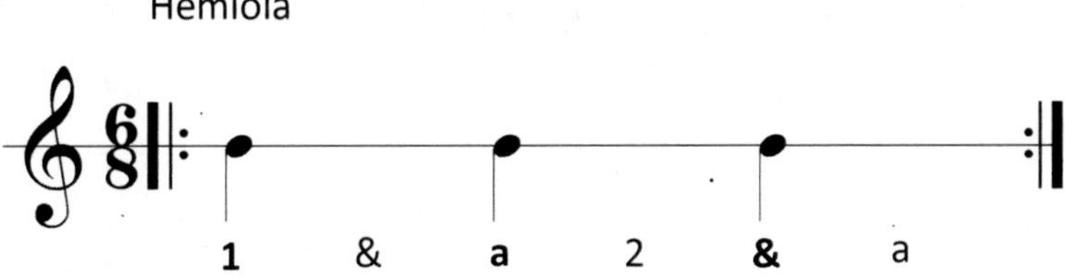

[17] For information on Indefinite Ties, see *Book 1*, p. 69.

Invention in F Major No. 3

AUDIO 29

21
25
B
29
34
38
1.
2.

The Key of D Minor

Shifting the tonic to D with the key signature of one flat is D natural minor. Observe the following whole/half step pattern:

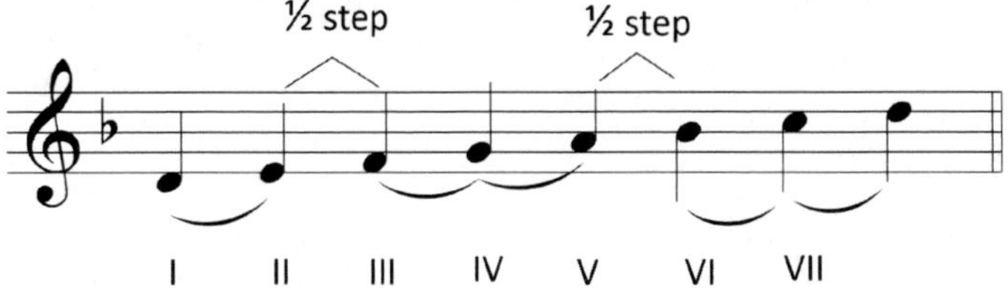

Review all of the open-position notes available in D natural minor, The A (la) in parenthesis will not be practiced in your scale, but is found in the music of this section.

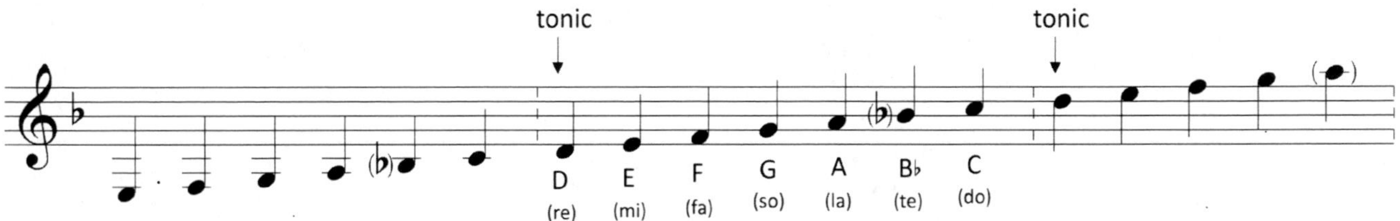

D Harmonic Minor

Adding the accidental C♯ (di) to D natural minor creates a leading tone and changes the mode to *harmonic minor*.

Pre-read, practice, and memorize the following scale.

- Practice vocalizing the names of the notes
- Find and touch all C♯ (di)'s.

D Melodic Minor

Adding accidentals B♮ (ti) and C♯ (di) raises the **VI** and **VII** degrees, changing the scale to D *melodic minor.* Pre-read, practice, and memorize the following scale.

Be able to play both harmonic and melodic minor scales, one stroke-per-note from memory.

Harmony

In the key of D minor, the tonic **I** chord is Dm and the dominant $\mathbf{V^7}$ is A^7.

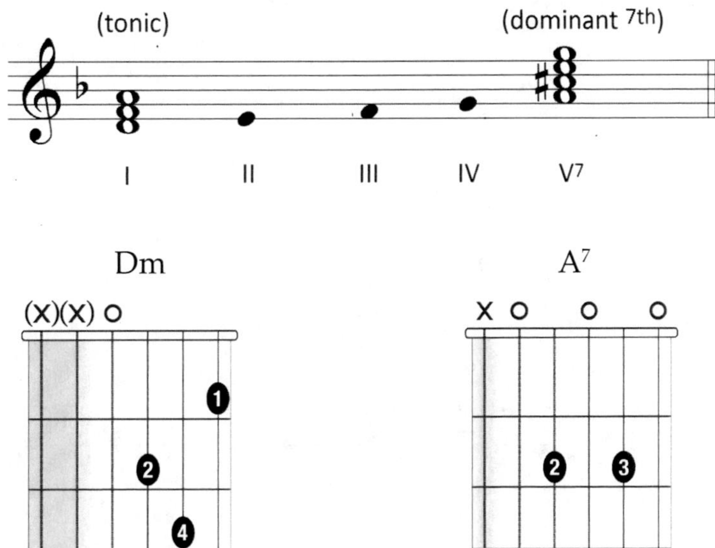

Practice strumming the D minor key progression.

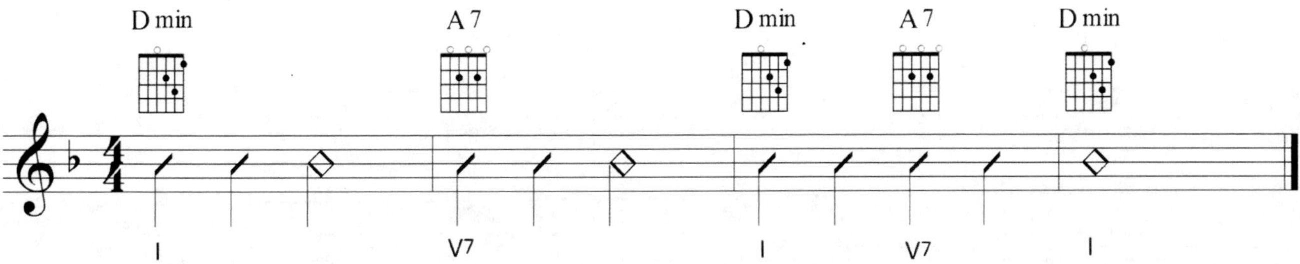

MIXED METER

So far, you've studied music written in a single meter, that is, with a time signature that remains steady throughout. But often in music written after the 19th century, meter may fluctuate with different time signatures, changing within the same phrase or throughout the piece. This is called *mixed meter*. Consider the following:

Counting the mixed-meter passage above, requires paying careful attention to the flux between $\frac{3}{4}$ and $\frac{2}{4}$. This metric irregularity may feel a little challenging at first, but can be mastered with patience and practice. When pre-reading mixed-metered music, immediately clarify the rhythm of the passage or line by counting aloud and clapping:

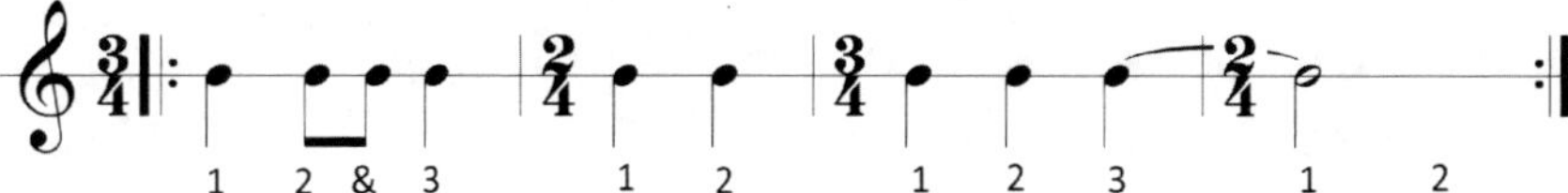

Your first introduction to mixed meter comes in *Invention in D Minor No.2* (p. 142) which is a rhythmic variation of the material in *D Minor No.1*.

Invention in D Minor No. 1

AUDIO 30

13
17
22
27
32
rit. . . . .

Invention in D Minor No. 2

AUDIO 31

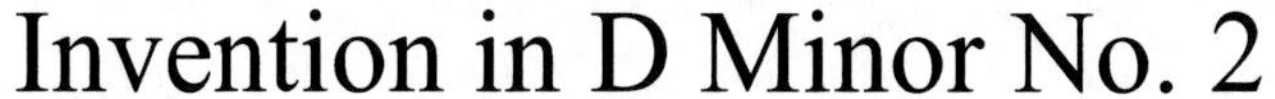

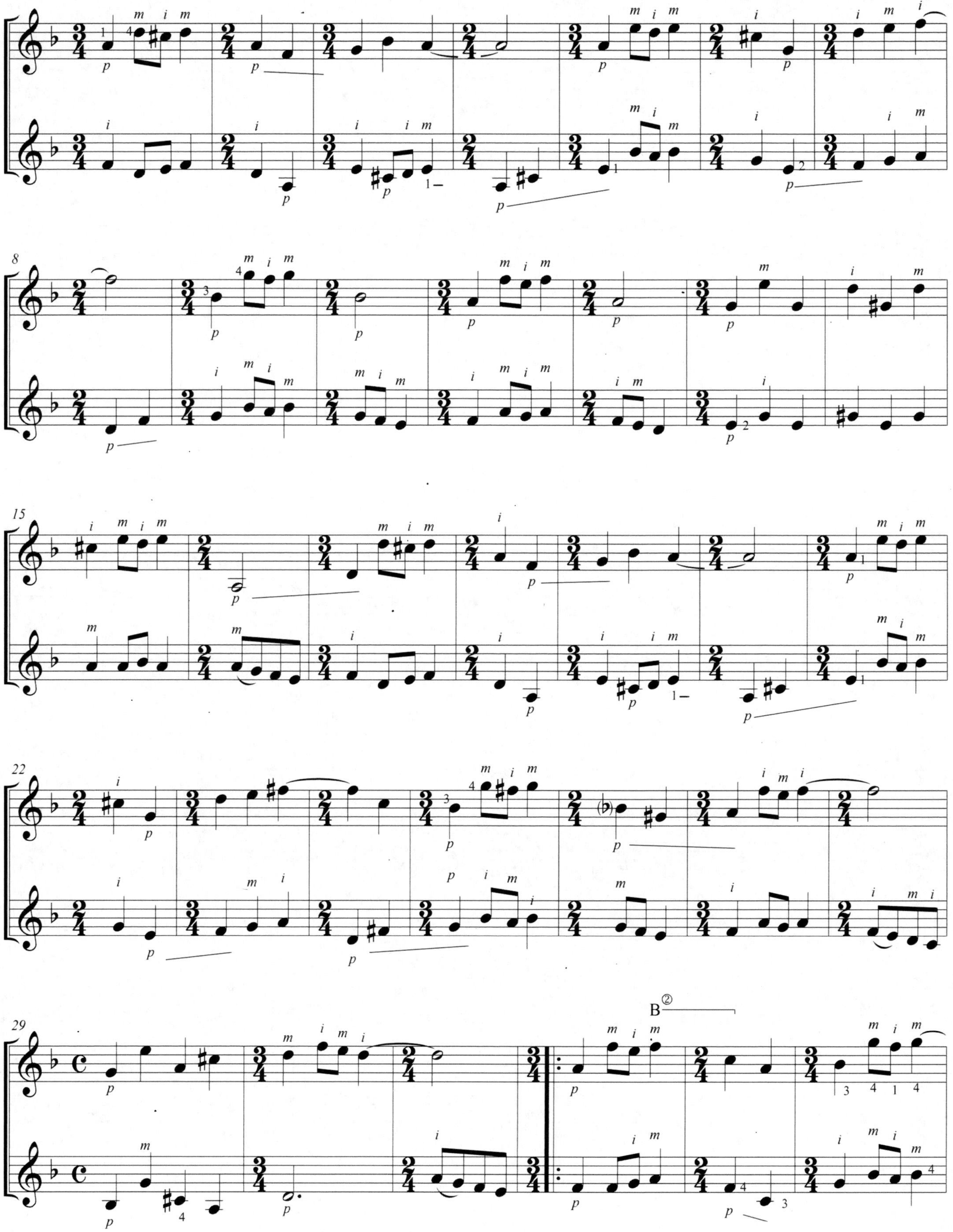

Invention in D Minor No. 3

AUDIO 32

21
25
29
33
37
rit. . . . .

Invention in D Minor No. 4

21
BII
26
BI
(BI)
BII
BII
31
BI
35
40
1.
2.

RHYTHM DANCE II—ALTERNATING COMPOUND AND SIMPLE METER

The following piece *Rhythm Dance II* begins with a mixed meter that alternates between compound $\frac{6}{8}$ and simple $\frac{2}{4}$. For both meters, the eighth note is constant, that is, it always sounds the same duration.

To better understand this, count aloud and clap Ex. 27a. Accent the numeric count as notated.

Ex. 27a - count and clap

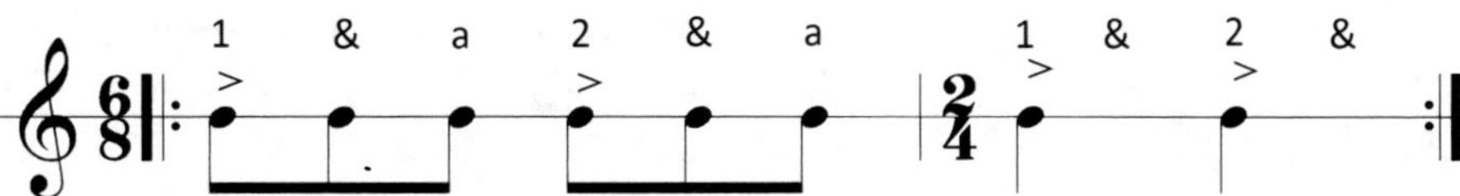

…next, apply the right-hand fingering, tapping the rhythmic pattern out on the soundboard. Continue counting.

Ex. 27b - tap on soundboard

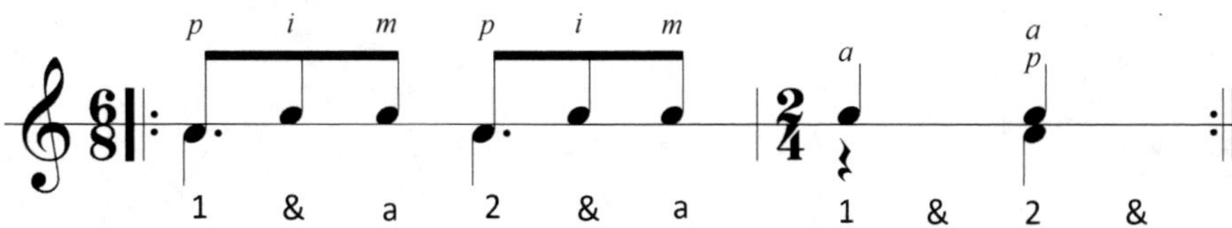

…finally transfer the rhythms to open strings, play and continue counting aloud:

Ex. 27c - play and count

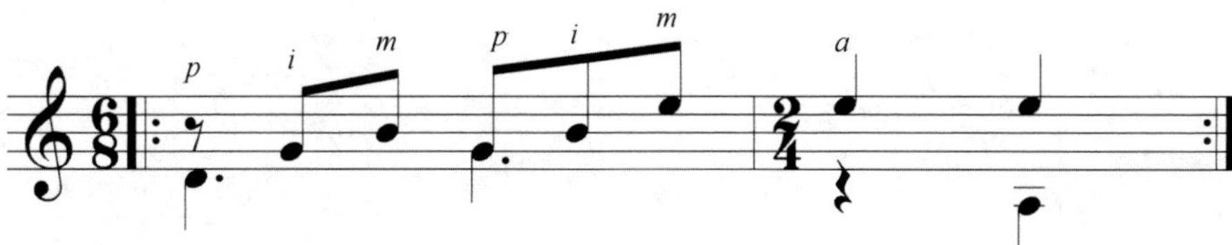

At m. 17, a different mixed-meter pattern of $\frac{3}{4}$ and $\frac{4}{4}$ is introduced.

Ex. 27d

Collapse the excerpt into a single rhythm and count aloud and clap.

Ex. 27e - count and clap

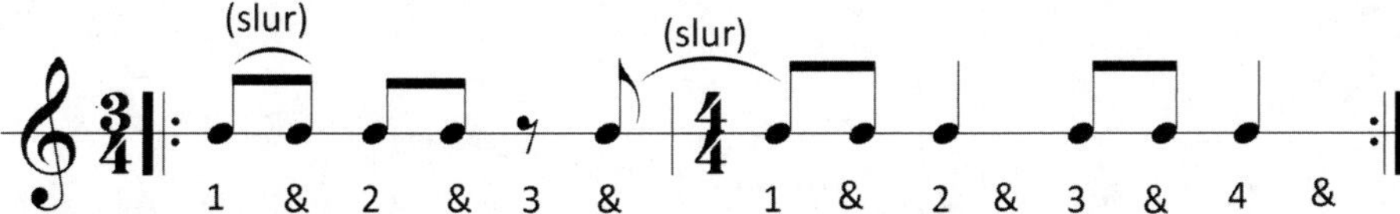

…next, transfer the rhythm to the open-strings, ignoring the slurred notes (since they are articulated by the left hand). Practice and count aloud until secure:

Ex. 27f - play and count

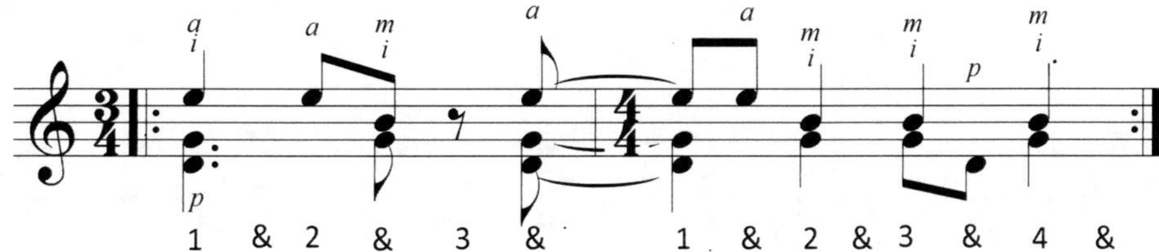

The last measure of *Rhythm Dance II* there is an indication for the chord to be strummed with the fingers.

Rhythm Dance II

AIM

The *a,i,m* arpeggio contains an opposed movement between *a* and *i* and a sympathetic movement between *m* and *a*. Prepare *i* as *a* flexes, and prepare *a-m* as *i* flexes. An effective way to approach the *a,i,m* arpeggio is first learn *i,m,a*.

- Establish the optimal position for *a* to sound ①.
- Prepare *i* on ③; *m-a* should be slightly flexed.
- Flex *i* to sound ③; as *i* flexes, prepare *m-a* on ② and ①.
- Flex *m* to sound ② and *a* sympathetically with *m* to sound ①.
- As *a* flexes, prepare *i* on ③.
- To play the *a,i,m* pattern, maintain the same organization and shift your start finger to *a* with *i* and *m* slightly flexed.

prepare a--
i,m slightly flexed
prepare i
prepare m,a
etc.
AIM
Arpeggio Study No. 2
rit.
a tempo
rit.

Motel Idaho

(AMI)

Arpeggio Study No. 3

SIMULTANEOUS REST/FREE STROKE

One very beautiful technique involves simultaneously playing rest-stroke fingers with a free- stroke thumb. Initially this can feel somewhat awkward due to the dissimilar sensations of each stroke. To allow your hand to adjust, be patient and proceed carefully. Begin with bass (free) and melody (rest) dyads.

- Make sure your hand is in a rest-stroke position.
- As you sound *p* free stroke and finger rest stroke, focus on the *simultaneous* attack of each.

In Ex. 28a, practice slowly and when possible, watch the right hand.

Ex. 28a

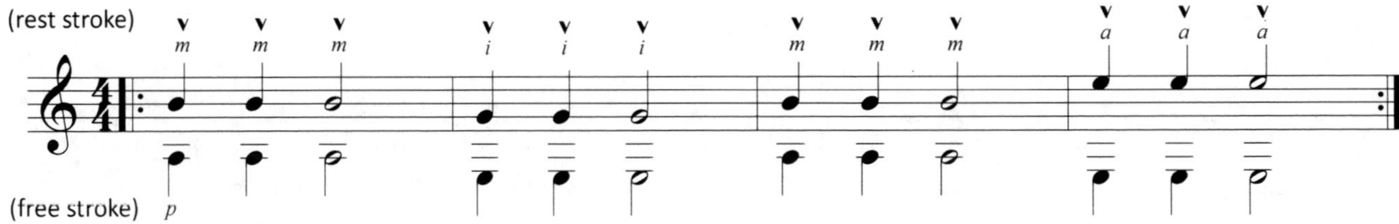

When secure with the above, practice simultaneous rest/free stroke with a simple second-position melody:

Ex. 28b

SIMULTANEOUS REST/FREE STROKE INVOLVING SCALAR PASSAGES

Often a situation arises where a rhythmically active rest-stroke melody is played against a free-stroke sustained bass. The following selection, *Volta* makes use of this technique. To prepare, practice on open strings in Ex. 29a.

Ex. 29a

Next, practice the same technique with a simple second-position melody:

Ex. 29b

Volta

WWW

During the pre-reading of *Volta*, pay particular attention to clarifying your right-hand requirements, if necessary each phrase or line at time. For example, consider the first four measures:

…next, realize the passage on open strings,

The section from mm. 9-16 should be played free stroke. Notice that it is also marked ponticello and that the melody in the bass is played with an alternation of *p* and *i*.

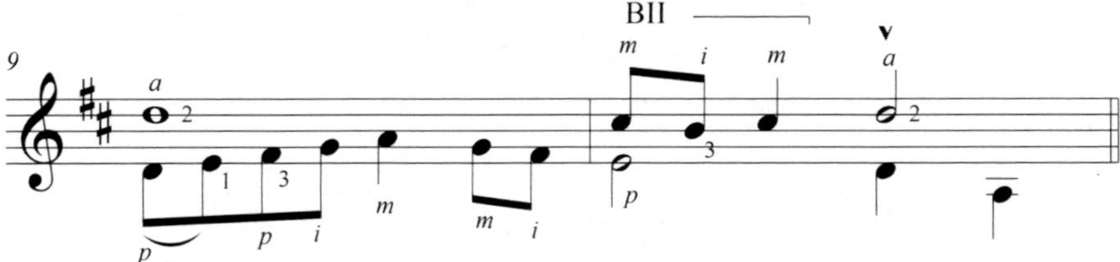

To coordinate the right hand, practice the passage realized as open strings:

Volta

ORNAMENTS

An *ornament* is a note or group of notes that decorates and gives life to a melody. The simplest of all ornaments is the *grace note*, a quick note written smaller than normal with a slash through its stem. Grace notes are played as fast as possible and usually slurred to the note they decorate.

grace note

Grace notes may precede a note either from above or below, either as a step or a skip. Practice each of the following types of grace notes, slurring each as quickly as possible to the longer quarter note:

Ex. 30a

The easiest way to play a grace note is on the beat. To play in tempo, begin by setting your metronome to about M.M.= 80. Count 4 ticks to establish the pulse and execute the slurred grace note directly on the beat. Practice until you've developed accuracy of aligning grace notes to beats:

Ex. 30b

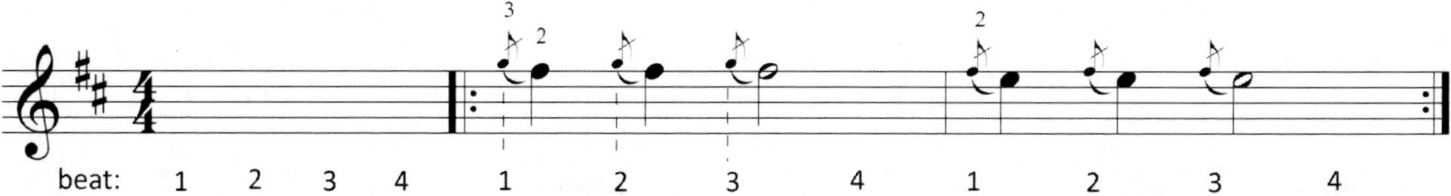

WWW

Next, practice the ornament while simultaneously sounding a bass note. While standard notation typically shows the grace note written slightly before the beat,

…it should always be played on the beat, simultaneous with *p*.

Ex. 30c

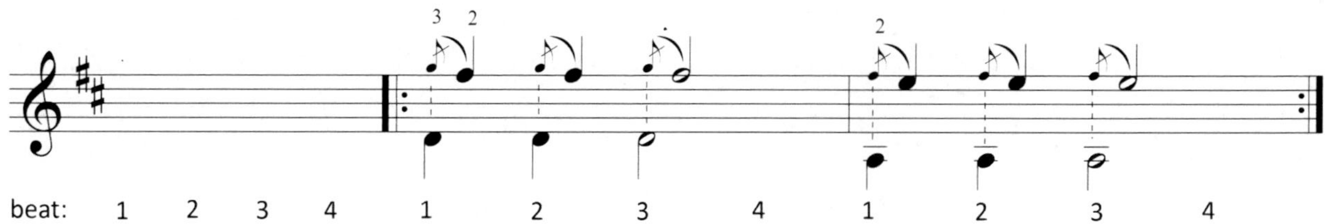

Trill

A *trill* is an ornament of at least two alternating adjacent notes. Like the grace note, it is written with smaller notation, should be played as fast as possible and is frequently slurred. The following is a two-note trill:

To play a two-note trill, simply move your left-hand finger as a quick, connected upward/downward slur (a hammer-on, pull-off combined movement). Practice the following:

Ex. 31a

Now play a two-note trill on the beat in steady rhythm. Begin by setting the metronome to about M.M.=80. Count 4 ticks to establish the pulse and execute the trill directly on the beat. Practice until you're able to accurately align trills to beats:

Ex. 31b

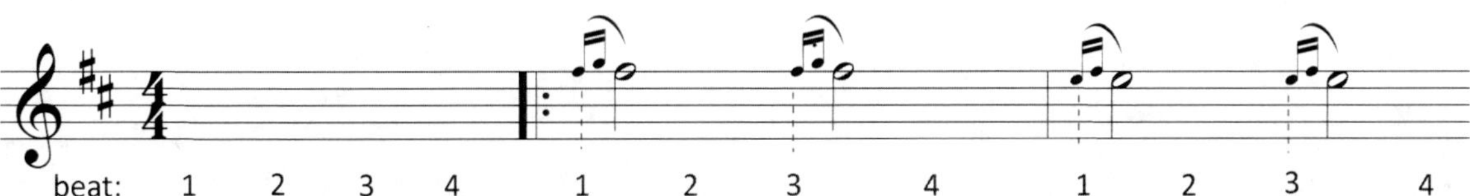

Finally, practice the trill while simultaneously playing a bass note. As in Ex. 30c, though the trill is written ahead of the beat,

...it should always be played simultaneously with *p*.

Ex. 31c

The following solo, *Gavotte*, provides practice in working with both grace notes and trills. As with *Volta*, the melody line should be played rest stroke where possible.

Gavotte

Moderately fast

SIMULTANEOUS REST/FREE STROKE—MELODY AND ACCOMPANIMENT

The simultaneous rest/free stroke technique is often used in a melody and accompaniment texture where free stroke is arpeggiated. To coordinate, practice on open strings in Exs. 32a and 32b:

Ex. 32a

Ex. 32b

Practice bringing out the simple melody in Ex. 32c:

Ex. 32c

Lyric Tune IV

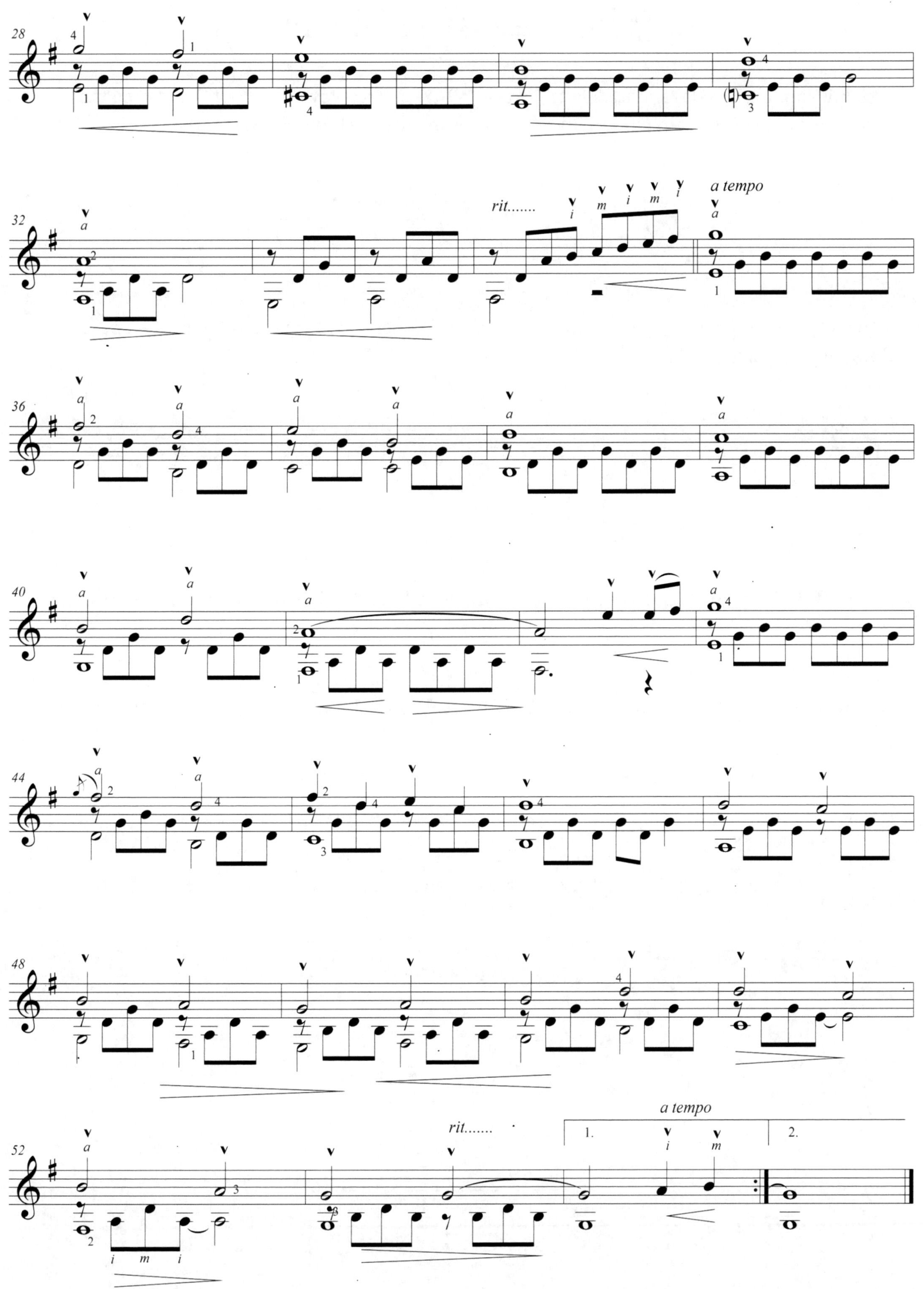
rit.......
a tempo
rit.......
a tempo
1.
2.

The Key of A Major

Establishing tonic A (la) and *leading tone* to G♯ (si) creates the key of *A major*. Following the necessary whole/half step pattern, the key signature now includes three sharps.

Review all open-position notes in the key A major. Notice the new note A (la) as the upper limit of pitch range.

Some of the A-major scale may be played with the left hand in Pos II, allowing you to reach A on ①.

Pre-read, practice, and memorize the following scale. Practice first with *free* and then with *rest stroke*.

- Vocalize note names and locate/touch all the leading-tone G♯ (si)'s.
- Begin slowly at first; when you can play the scale securely, accelerate the tempo, but continue to play without hesitation.
- When secure, be able to play the scale one stroke-per-note from memory.

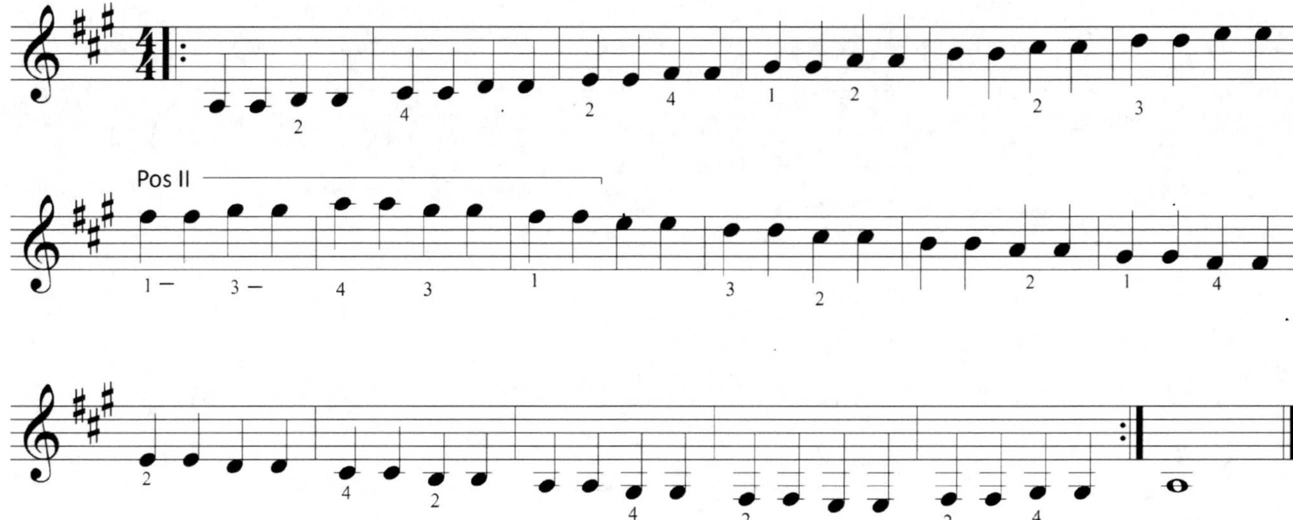

Harmony

In the key of A major, the **I** is A and the **V**^{7} chord is E^7.

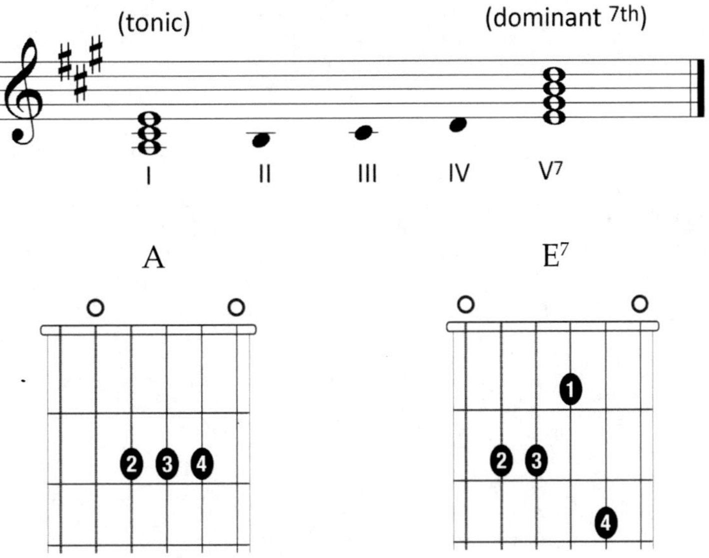

Practice strumming the key progression:

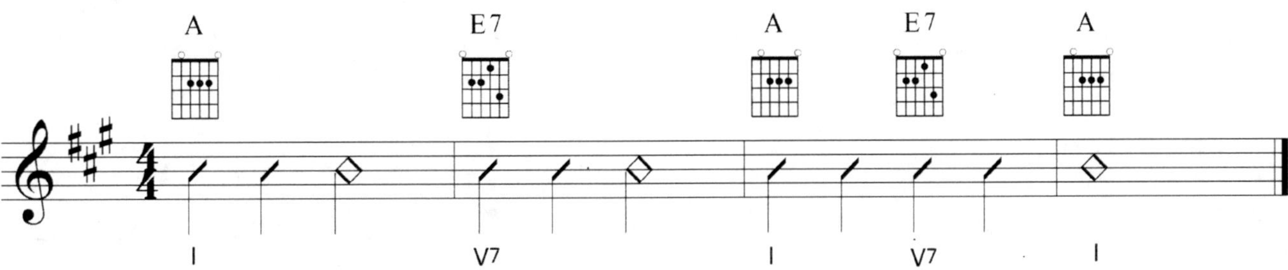

IRREGULAR METER

Another example of meter found in music after the 19th century is *irregular meter,* organized into asymmetrical groupings of beats, such as 5, or 7. Following are examples of typical irregular meters:

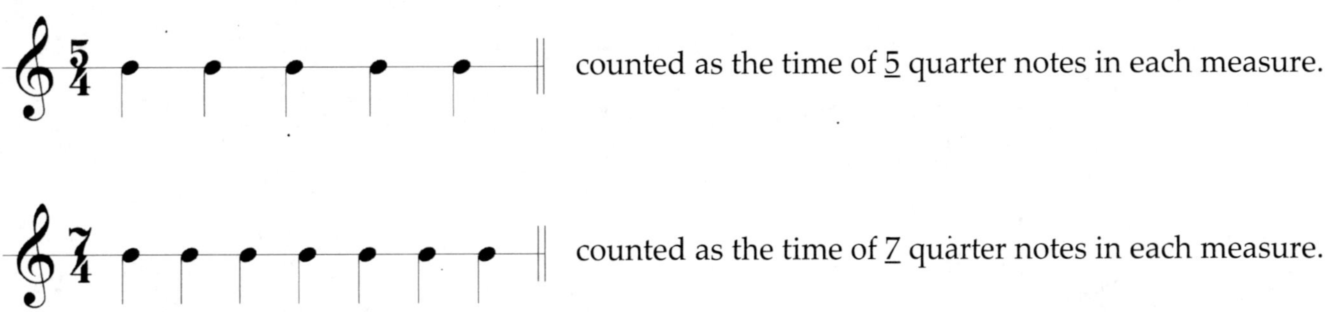

The following *Invention In A Major No. 1* is written in $\frac{5}{4}$. Carefully pre-read before playing.

Invention in A Major No. 1

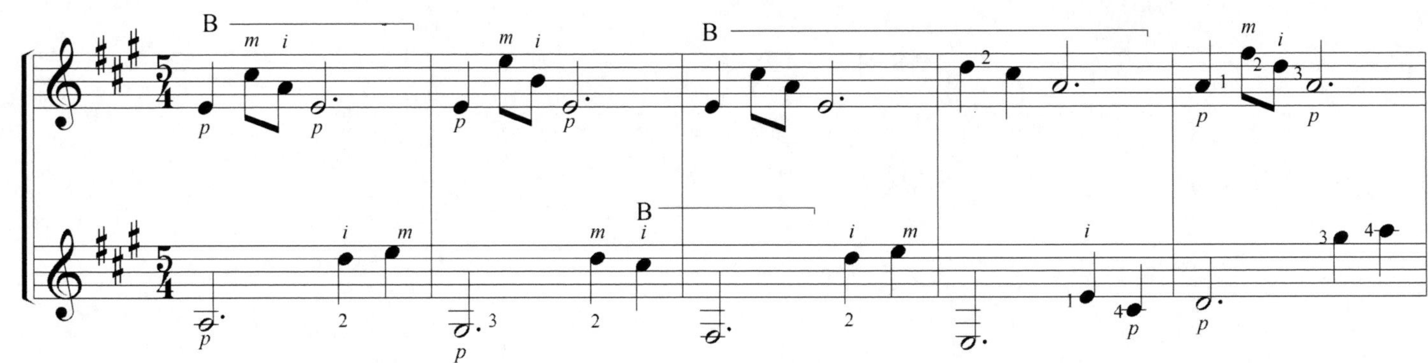

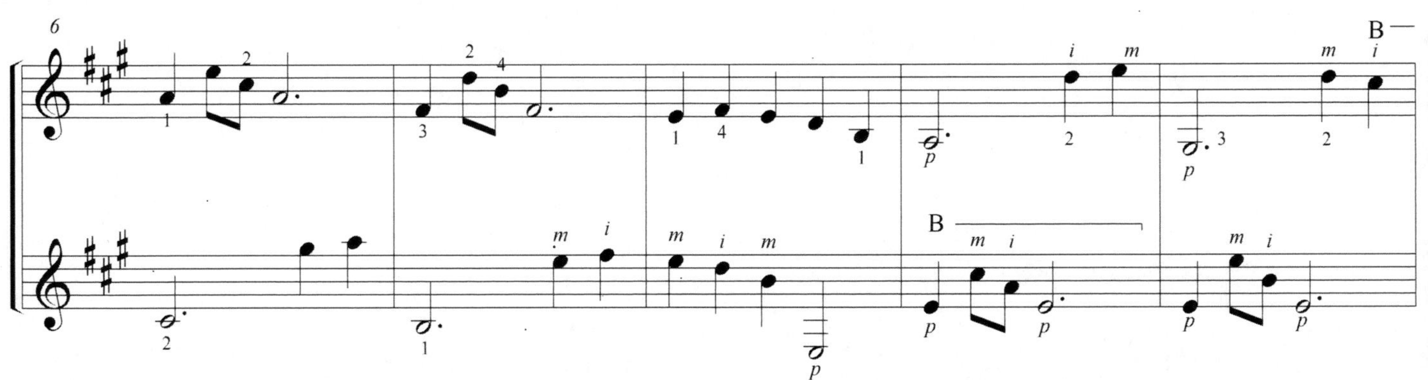

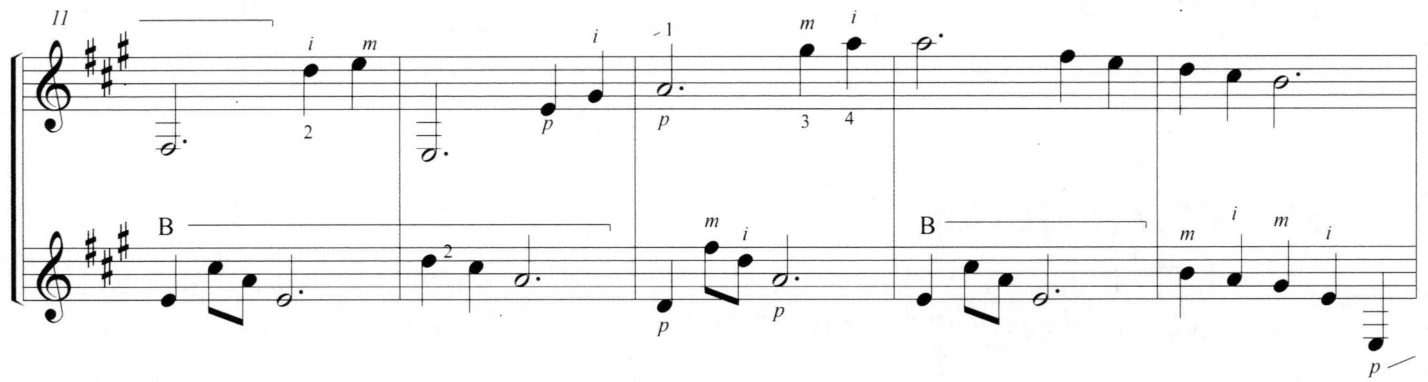

rit. . . . .
a tempo

Invention in A Major No. 2

AUDIO 35

19
22
25
28
31
rit. . . . .
B

Invention in A Major No. 3

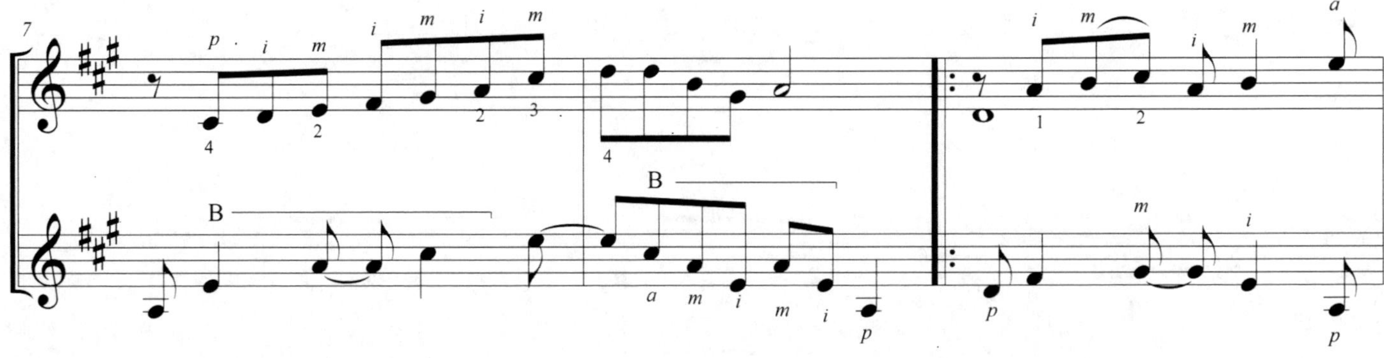

rit. . . . .
a tempo
(2x ritard)

Invention in A Major No. 4

AUDIO 37

rit. . . .
a tempo
(2x ritard)

The Key of F♯ Minor

The relative of A is F♯ minor with a key signature of three sharps. Below is the minor scale's whole-/half-step pattern.

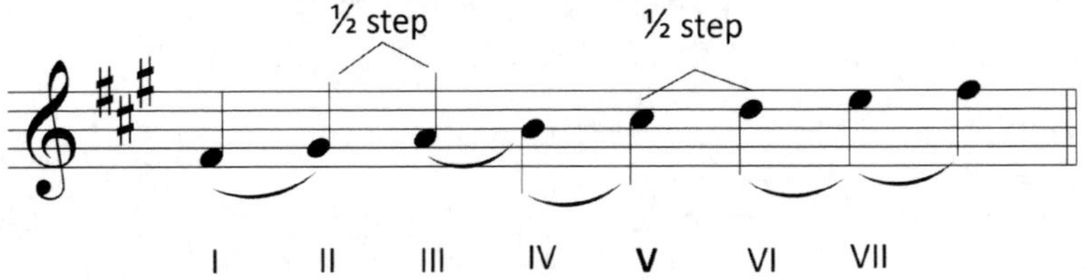

F♯ Natural Minor Scale

Review all of the open-position notes available in F♯ natural minor. Notice also the A (la) on A

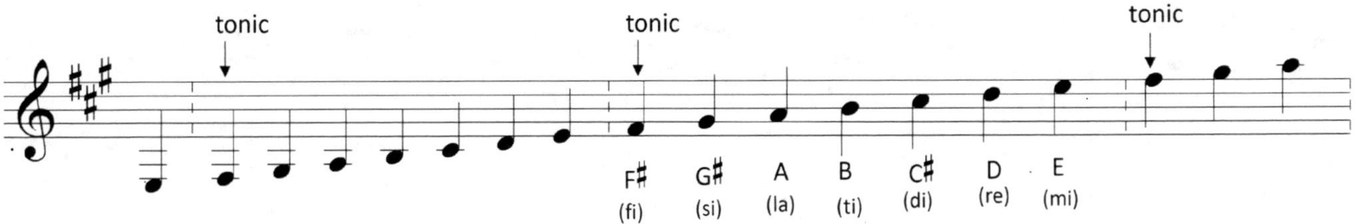

WWW

F♯ Harmonic Minor

Pre-read, practice, and memorize the following F♯ *harmonic minor* scale.

- Vocalize all note names and locate/touch all the leading-tone E♯'s (*my*).
- Begin slowly at first; when you can play the scale securely, accelerate the tempo, but continue to play without hesitation

F♯ Melodic Minor

Adding accidentals D♯ (*di*) and E♯ (*my*) raises the **VI** and **VII** degrees, changing the scale to F♯ *melodic minor.* As in the harmonic minor form of the scale, there is a temporary shift in and out Pos II to accommodate the A on ①. Pre-read and memorize the following *F♯ melodic minor* scale.

Be able to play both harmonic and melodic minor scales, one stroke-per-note from memory.

Harmony

In the key of F♯ minor, **I** is F♯m and **V**^{7} is C♯^{7}.

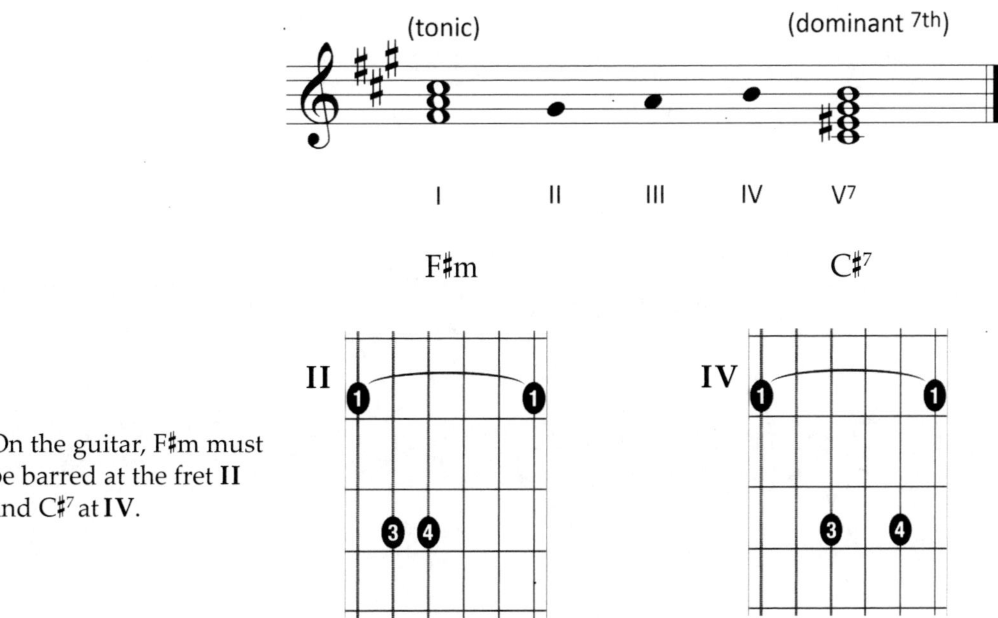

On the guitar, F♯m must be barred at the fret **II** and C♯^{7} at **IV**.

Practice strumming the F♯ minor key progression:

Invention in F♯ Minor No. 1

AUDIO 38

20
BII
(BI ③)
23
BII
26
29
BII
BII
33
1
2

WWW

Invention in F♯ Minor No. 2

AUDIO 39

*(H.B.)

* Hinge Bar--see WWW

21
25
28
31
34
rit. . . . .
B

Invention in F♯ Minor No. 3

AUDIO 40

26
B
31
36
41
B
46
1
2
B

A,M,I,M

The *a,m,i,m* arpeggio consists of two alternations and two sympathetic movements. Prepare two fingers at a time: *i-m* when *a* flexes, and *m-a* when *i* flexes. As always, *c* should move with *a*. Proceed as follows:

- Position *a* for optimal leverage.
- Prepare *a* on ①; *i-m* should be slightly flexed.
- Flex *a* to sound ①; as *a* flexes, simultaneously prepare *i-m* on ③ and ②.
- Flex *m* sympathetically with *a* to sound ②.
- Flex *i* to sound ③; as *i* flexes, simultaneously prepare *m-a* on ② and ①.
- Flex *m* sympathetically with *i* to sound ②.

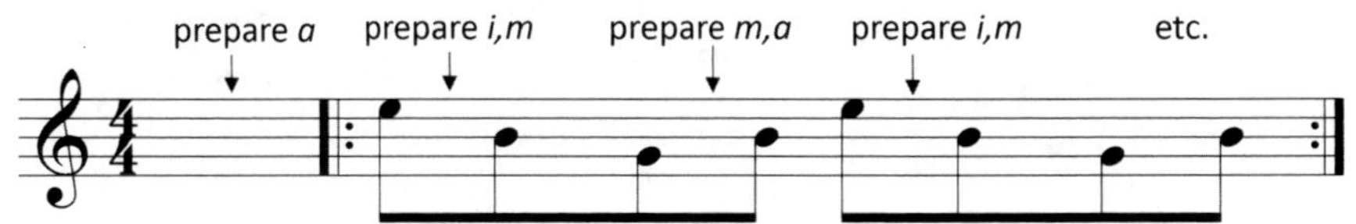

Now proceed with the AMIM selection (p. 183).

I,A,M,A

The *i,a,m,a* arpeggio also consists of two alternations and one sympathetic movement.

- Prepare *i* on ③; *m-a* should be slightly flexed.
- Flex *i* to sound ③; as *i* flexes, prepare *m-a* on ② and ①.
- Flex *a* to sound ①.
- Flex *m* sympathetically to sound ②; as *m* flexes, prepare *a* on ①.
- Flex *a* sympathetically with *m* to sound ①; as *a* flexes, prepare *i* on ③.

Notice the two alternations, and the single sympathetic movement: an alternation between *i* and *a-m*, an alternation between *a* and *m*, and a sympathetic movement between *m* and *a*.

Now proceed with the IAMA selection (p. 184).

AMIM

Arpeggio Study No. 4

IAMA

Arpeggio Study No. 5

GLISSANDO

Another type of left-hand articulation is the *glissando*. It's produced by sliding a depressed finger either up or down along a string to produce a change in pitch. Depending on the expressive needs of the music, glissandos may be played in various ways: quickly, slowly, or in a steady and even rhythm (see the DVD). To feel glissando in a steady rhythm, carefully practice the following examples.

Ascending Glissando

Begin by playing and counting aloud. Ex. 33a with no glissando. Once secure with the fingering and rhythmic patterns, begin Ex. 33b with the glissando. Here your goal is to move "3" evenly along ④ with the same steady count as Ex. 33a.

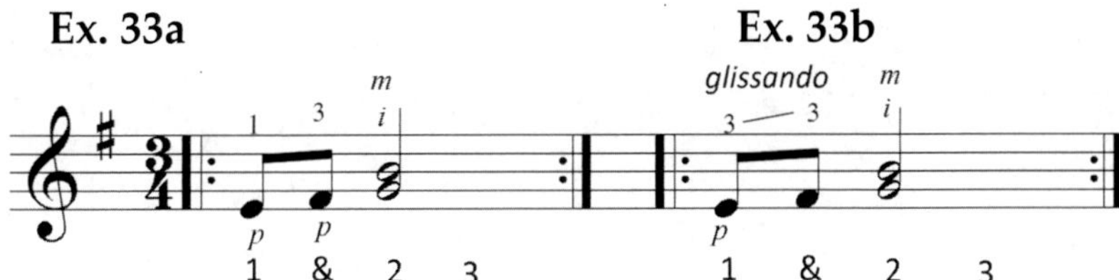

Descending Glissando

To begin, play and count aloud. Ex. 34a, with no glissando. When you feel secure with the fingering and rhythmic patterns, apply the glissando as notated in Ex. 34b. As before, your goal is to move "2" evenly along ④ with the same steady count as Ex. 34a.

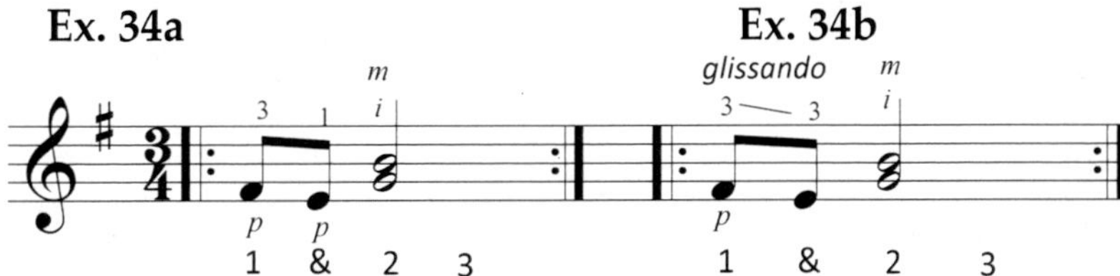

Ascending and Descending Glissandos

With your metronome set <u>slowly</u>, practice the following glissandos in a steady, even rhythm. Note the keys signature of 2 sharps.

Ex. 35

E on ②

The following solo, *Saturday Mornin'*, includes E (mi) on ② at fret V. In addition, you'll find occasional glissandos as well as both the *a,m,i,m* and *i,a,m,a* arpeggios without *p*.

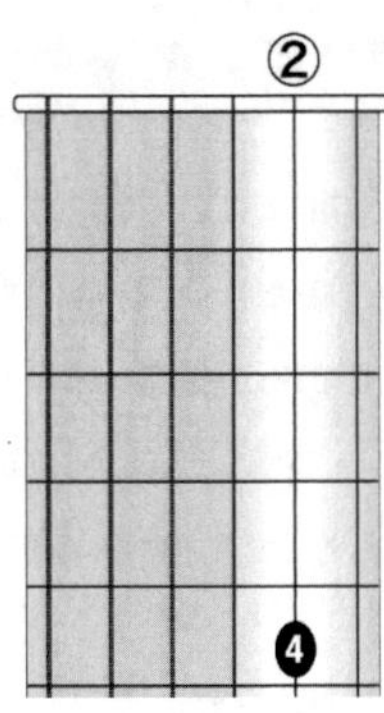

Saturday Mornin'

In the following solo, *Either or…*, be sure to play the glissando rhythmically even. Notice the campanella texture beginning at m. 17.

Either or...

GRACE-NOTE GLISSANDOS

Another way of expressing a glissando is as a grace note, played very fast and often occurring just before the beat. With you metronome set <u>slowly,</u> practice playing grace-note glissandos, making sure that the quarter note occurs directly on the beat:

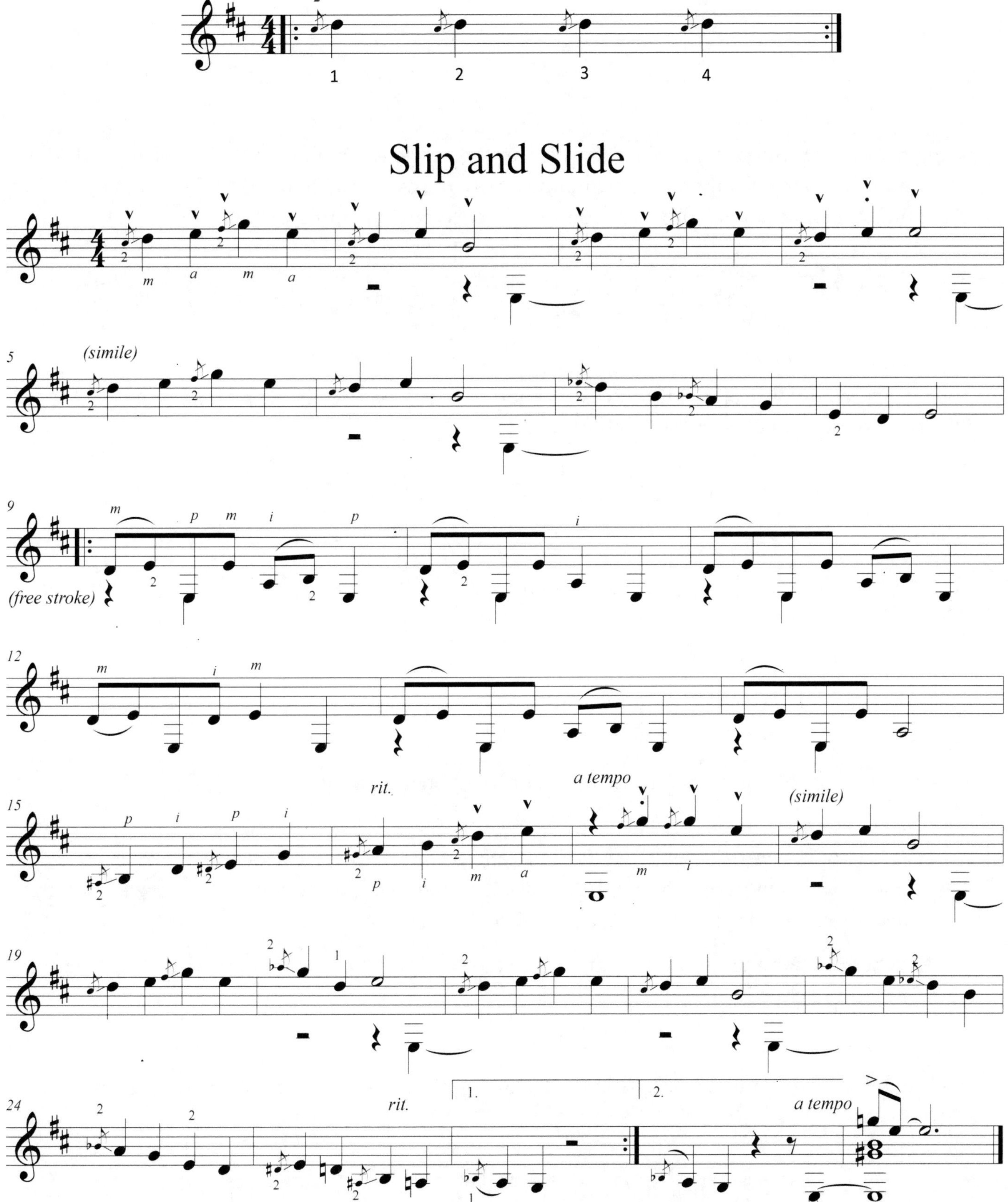

D' BLUES—BENDING AND STRUMMING

Grace-note glissandos are found in the following solo, *D'Blues*. The piece also includes a few new techniques starting with an optional *string bend* at m. 20:

String bending requires that the left-hand finger flex while remaining on the fret. This pulls the string out of its normal alignment and momentarily raises the pitch. Bends are notated as ↗, indicating to bend the pitch upward. You can practice pitch bending below:

The final measure of *D'Blues* introduces another new technique called rapid strumming (or *rasgueado*) which appears on the A^7 chord:

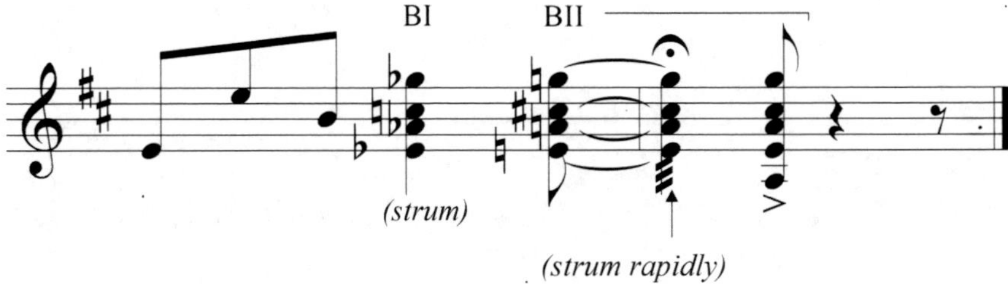

Rapid strumming, notated as ≣, may be interpreted in a variety of ways. One of the easiest is as follows:

- Place *p* on either ⑤ or ⑥ to anchor your hand on the guitar.
- Rapidly move the tip of *i* back and forth over strings ①, ②, ③, and ④. You should sense the movement principally coming from the *i* basal and middle joints. Strumming from bass to treble string is called a *downstroke* (↓); from treble to bass is called an *upstroke* (↑).

- While strumming, count the duration of the chord and end with a downstroke on the following chord.

Practice rapid strumming technique in the following (with a downward strum on the 3rd beat):

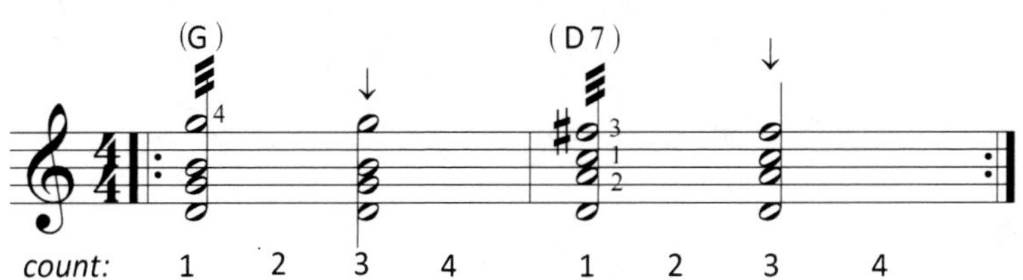

D' Blues

* optional bend

Reflection

* optional grace note

19
m a
i
B
22
i m a
rit. . .
a tempo
25
m i
a m
28
31
i
p i a
34
1
i m a m
2
rit. . .

RHYTHM DANCE III – $\frac{5}{8}$

Rhythm Dance III is written in an asymmetrical $\frac{5}{8}$ meter, meaning the time of 5 eighth notes in each measure, or: $\frac{5}{♪}$

The best way to count $\frac{5}{8}$ is not as 5 eighth-note beats, but in 2 beats—as one *simple* and one *compound,* or vice versa. Alternating between compound and simple beats is similar in feeling to the mixed meter in *Rhythm Dance II,* though more quickly juxtaposed.

Ex. 36a - count and clap

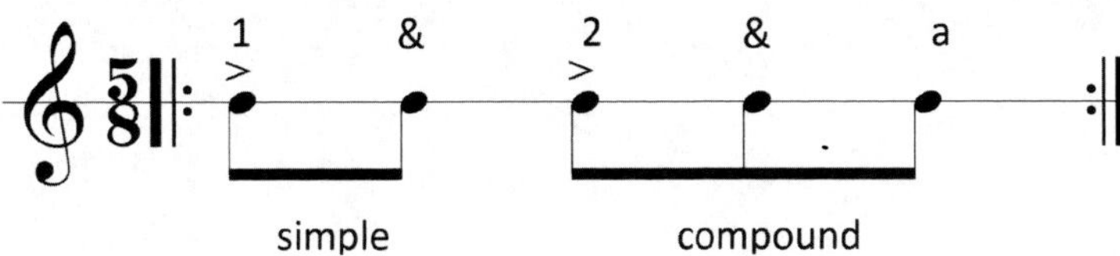

Ex. 36b - count and clap

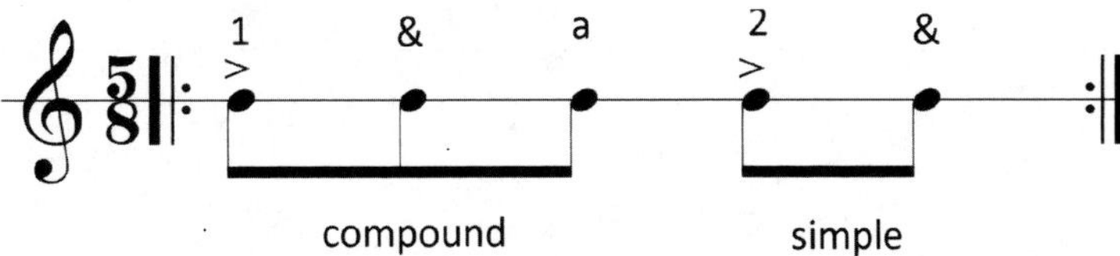

Clap and count aloud the measures above, giving stress to the numerical beats. Practice slowly and compare the different accent patterns between the two measures:

The $\frac{5}{8}$ pattern found in *Ryhthm Dance III* is the latter combination—one compound beat and one simple beat. The pattern is shown below. Begin be counting aloud and tapping on the soundboard. Stems down indicates thumb and stem up indicates fingers:

Ex. 36c - tap on soundboard

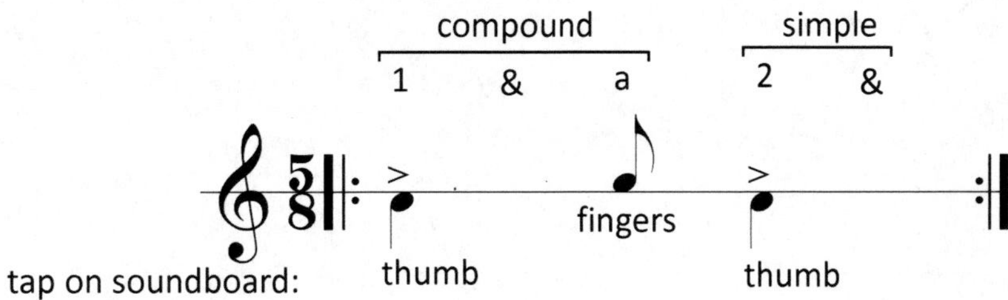

Next transfer the rhythmic feeling to open strings and continue to count aloud. Practice until secure:

Ex. 36d - play and count

When pre-reading *Rhythm Dance III,* watch for the glissando on ④ at m. 8. If necessary isolate Begin slowly at first; when secure, accelerate the tempo without hesitation.

Ex. 36e

Rhythm Dance III

a tempo
glissando
rit. . . . .

Tanglewood is written in mixed meter and includes measures of $\frac{5}{8}$. Be sure to carefuly clarify the rhythm and counting when pre-reading.

Tanglewood

RHYTHM DANCE IV—$\frac{7}{8}$

Rhythm Dance IV is written in $\frac{7}{8}$, meaning the time of 7 quarter notes in each measure: $\frac{7}{♪}$

Rather than counting in 7, count in 3 beats—as two *simple* and one *compound*, or vice versa. The feeling is similar to $\frac{5}{8}$ with an added simple beat.

Clap and count aloud the following, stressing the numerical beats. Practice slowly, listening in each measure to the different accent patterns.

Ex. 37a - count and clap

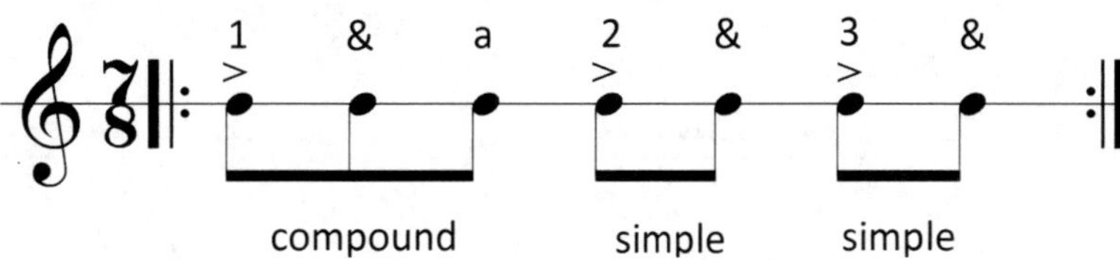

Ex. 37b - count and clap

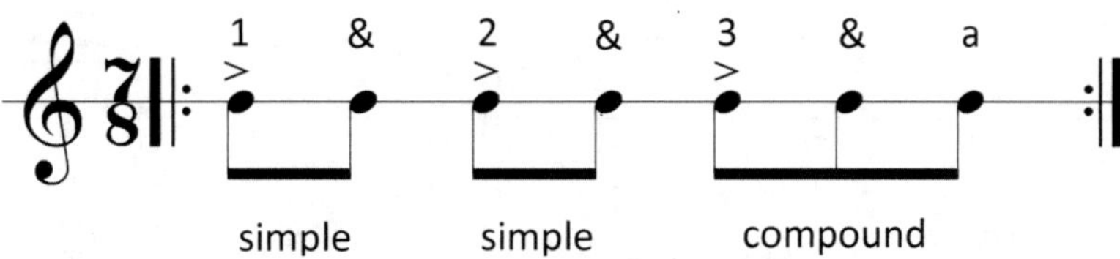

The principal pattern found in *Ryhthm Dance IV* is the latter combination—two simple beats and one compound beat as shown below.

Ex. 37c - count and clap

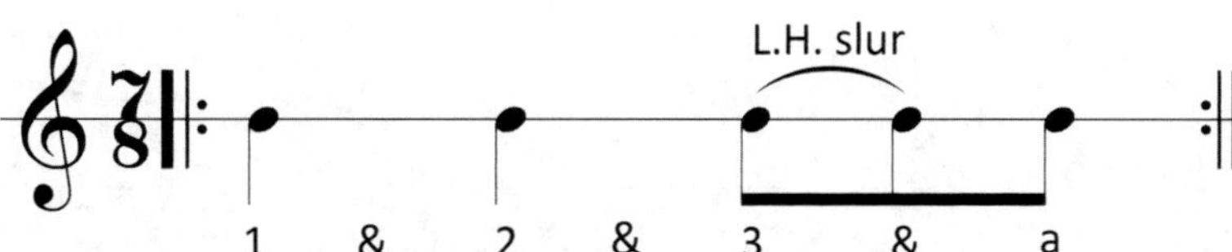

Notice the left-hand slur on count <u>3&</u>. When transfering this rhythm for the right hand only, the eighths are combined as a one quarter. Tap on the soundboard and count aloud the following:

Ex. 37d - tap on soundboard

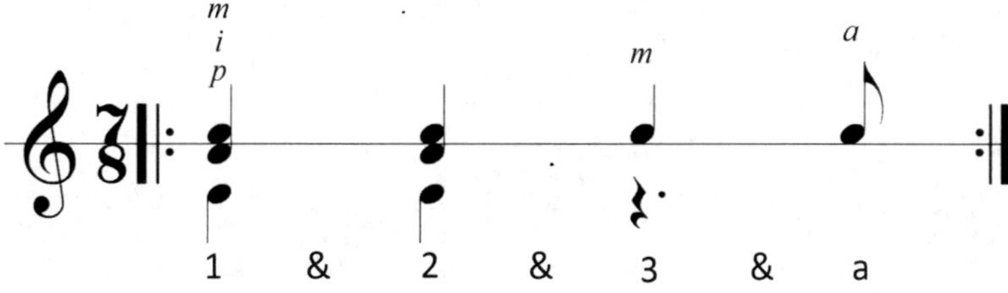

Now continue to count aloud and practice the passage on open strings:

Ex. 37e - play and count

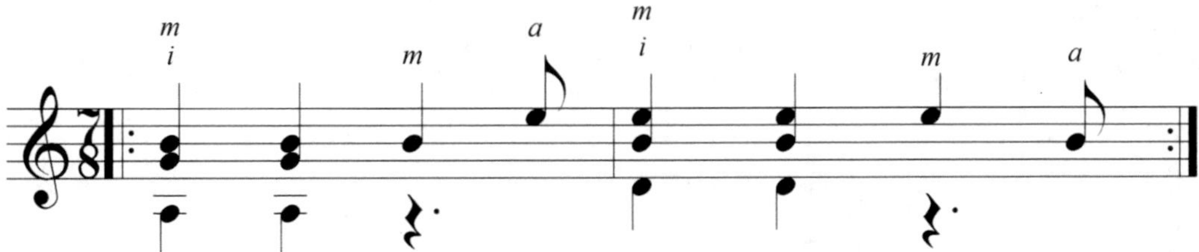

When pre-reading *Rhythm Dance IV,* watch for the occasional glissando on ④. Its rhythmic position, on the same count as the slur—3&—maintains the same rhythmic pattern as in Ex. 37e.

Ex. 37f

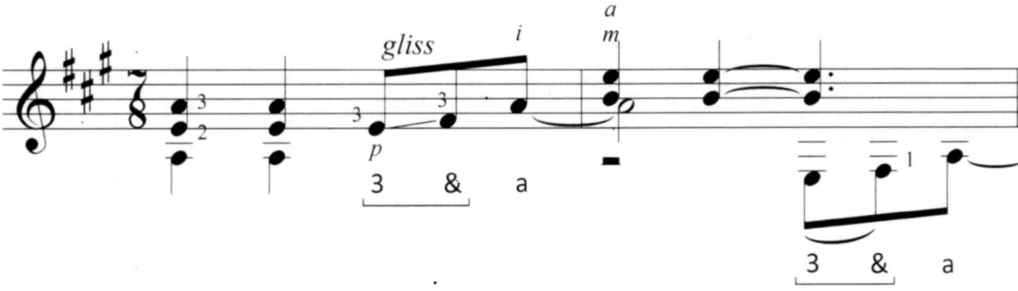

Ex. 37g - tap on soundboard

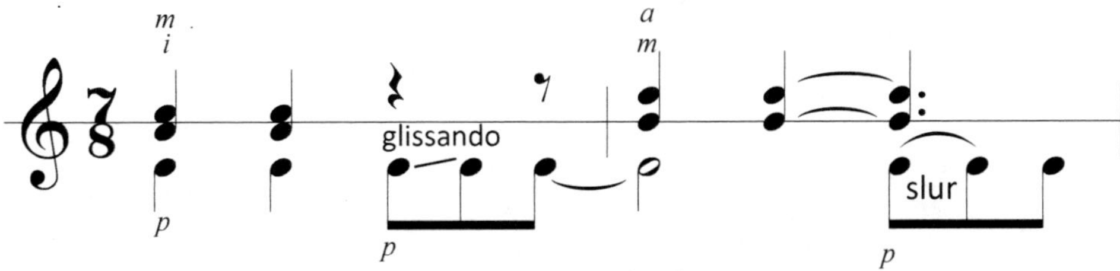

Rhythm Dance IV

gliss
gliss
B④
B④

The Key of E Major

Establishing tonic E (mi) and *leading tone* to D♯ (ri) creates the key of *E major*. The key signature now includes four sharps (F♯, C♯, G♯, D♯) giving way to the correct whole/half step pattern:

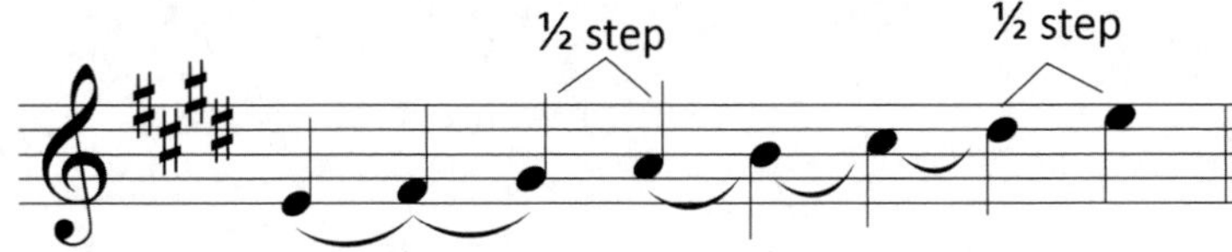

Review all open-position notes in the key E major. Notice note A (la) as the upper limit of pitch range.

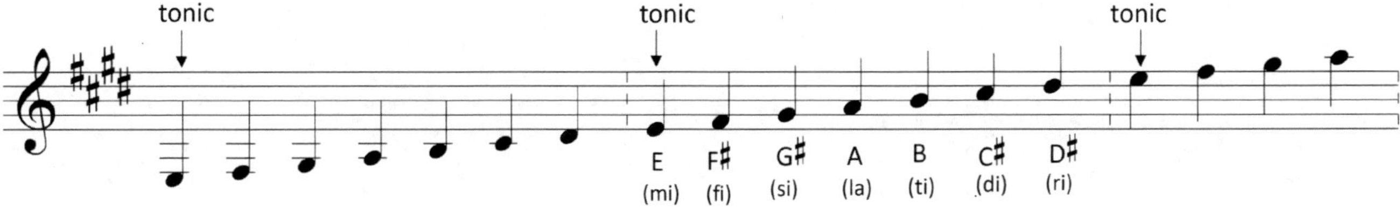

To reach A on ①, the E-major scale will temporarily be played with the left hand in Position II.

Pre-read, practice, and memorize the following scale. Practice first with *free* and then with *rest stroke*.

- Vocalize note names.
- Begin slowly at first; when secure, accelerate the tempo without hesitation.
- When secure, be able to play the scale one stroke-per-note from memory.

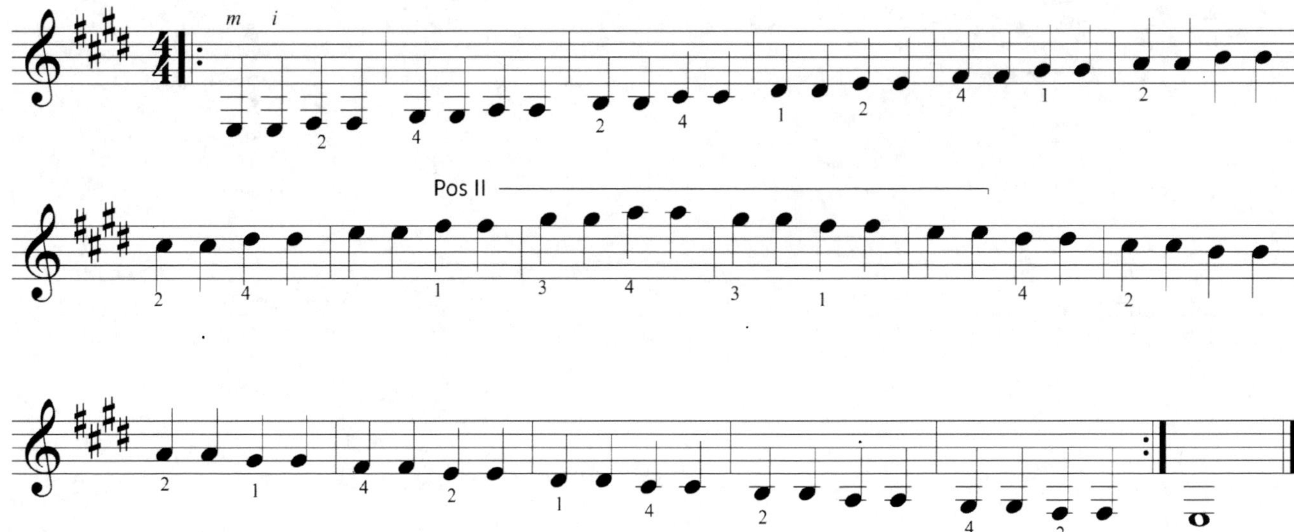

Harmony

In the key of E Major, the **I** is E and the **V**^{7} chord is B^7.

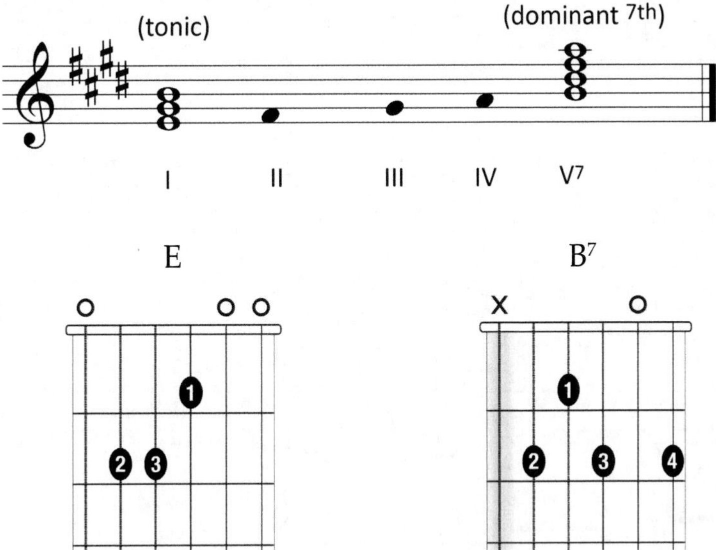

Practice strumming the key progression:

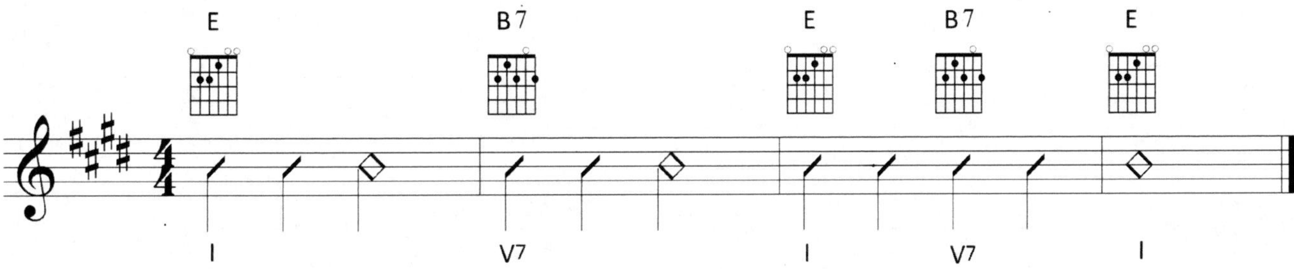

Invention in E Major No. 3

As always, free stroke should be used when playing passages involving alternation between adjacent strings as in *Invention in E Major No. 3* (p. 210). In addition, this allows each stem down voice to sustain for a full quarter note:

Invention in E Major No. 1

AUDIO 41

16
20
24
28
B
31
1.
2.
rit. . . . .

Invention in E Major No. 2

a tempo
(gliss)
rit. . . . .
rit. . . . .
1.
2.
B

Invention in E Major No. 3

AUDIO 43

move to ord.
rit. . . . .

A,I,M,I

This is the final arpeggio without *p*. In this pattern, there are no sympathetic movements with subsequent sounding strings: it consists entirely of alternations between *i* and *m-a*. Always move *m-a* together in this movement, but only prepare the one that is about to sound a string.

AIMI

Arpeggio Study No. 6

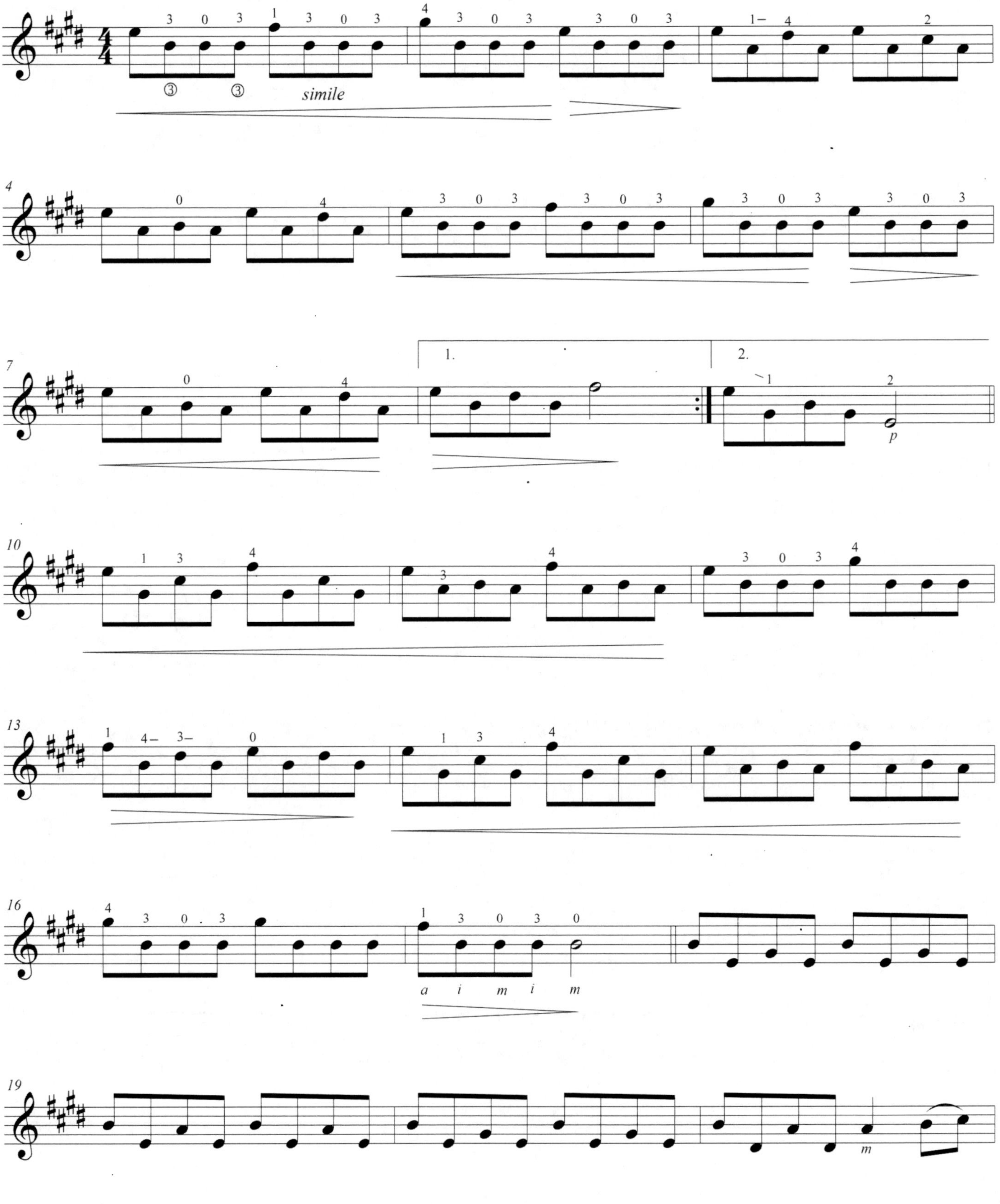

simile

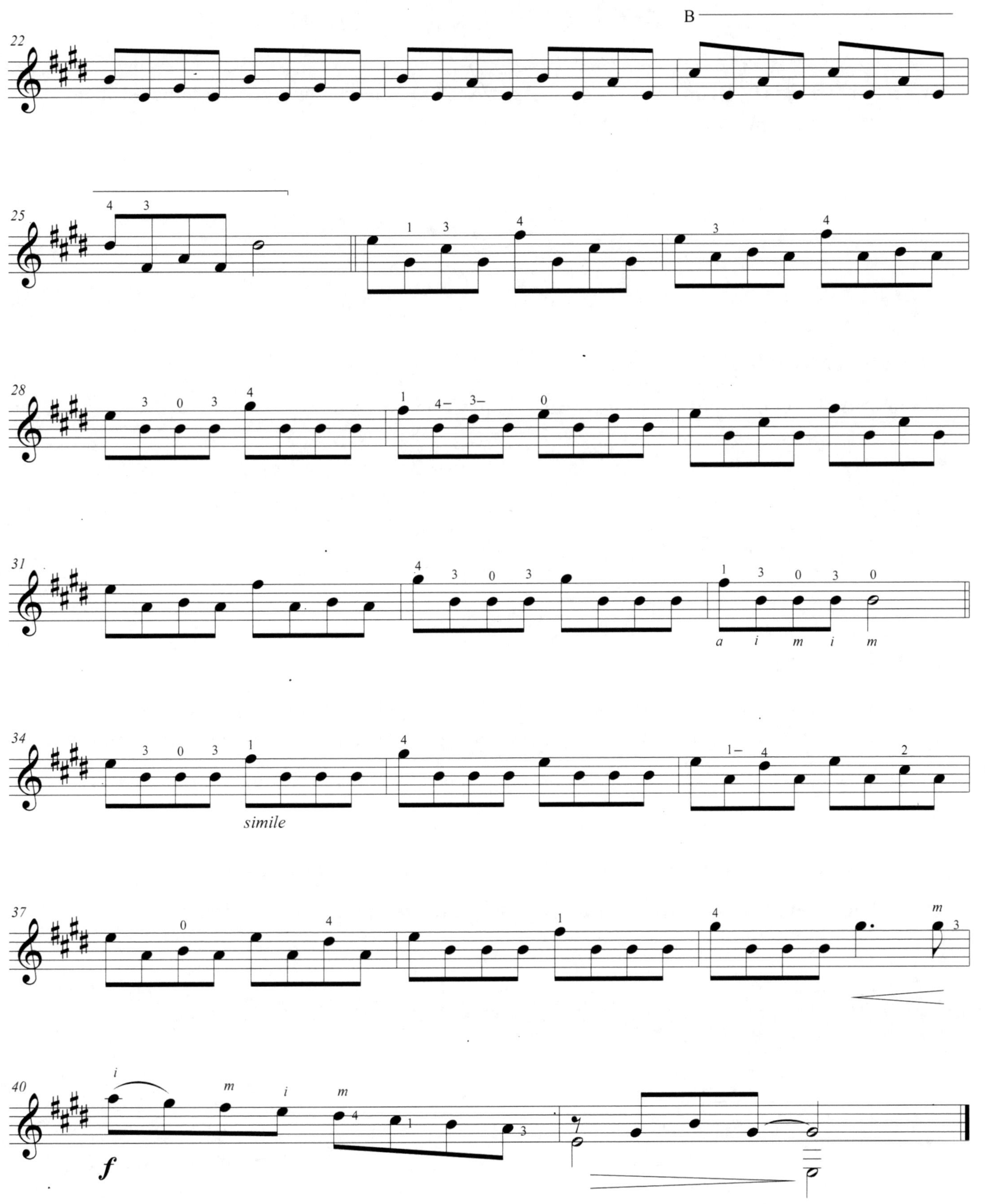

B
simile
a i m i m
f

The Key of C♯ Minor

The relative of E is C♯ minor with a key signature of four sharps. Below is the minor scale's whole-/half-step pattern.

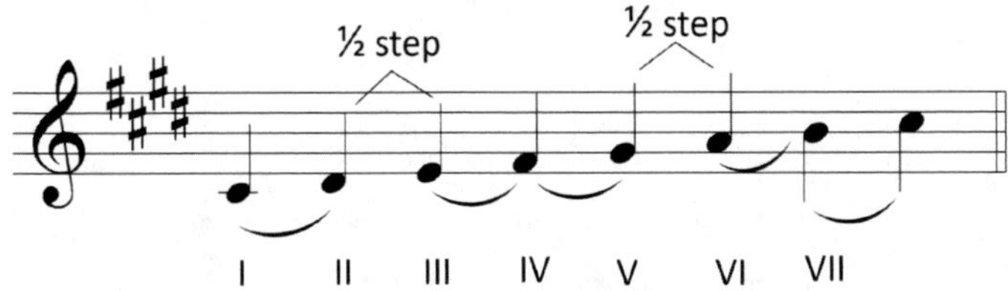

C♯ Natural Minor Scale

Review all of the open-position notes available in C♯ natural minor:

C♯ Harmonic Minor

Adding the accidental B♯ (ty) to C♯ natural minor creates a leading tone and changes the mode to *harmonic minor*. Though enharmonic with C, B♯ must be used to maintain scalar appearance.

In order to include A on ① in scale, the left hand will temporarily shift in and out of Pos II.

Pre-read, practice, and memorize the following C♯ *harmonic minor* scale.

- Vocalize all note names and locate/touch all the leading-tone B♯ (*ty*)'s.
- Begin slowly at first; when secure, accelerate the tempo without hesitation

C♯ Melodic Minor

Adding accidentals A♯ (li) and B♯ (ty) raises the **VI** and **VII** degrees, changing the scale to C♯ *melodic minor.* Pre-read, practice, and memorize the following *C♯ melodic minor* scale.

Be able to play both harmonic and melodic minor scales, one stroke-per-note from memory.

Harmony

In the key of C♯ minor, **I** is C♯m and **V**^{7} is G♯^{7}.

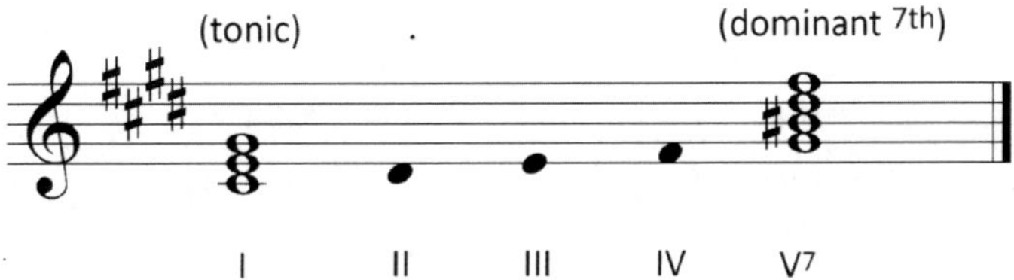

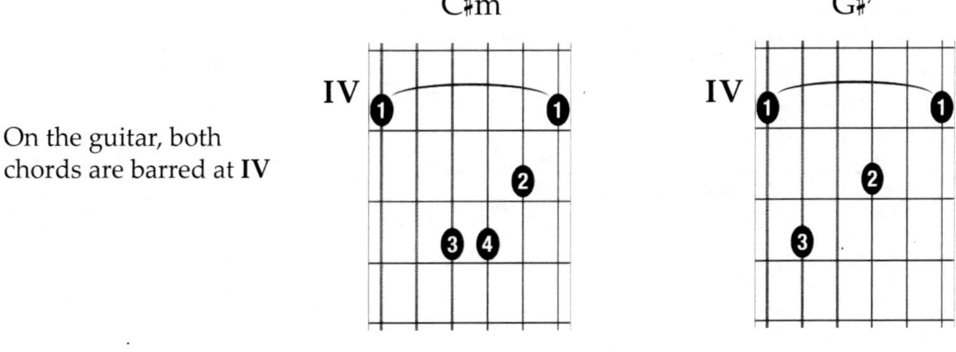

On the guitar, both chords are barred at **IV**

Practice strumming the key progression:

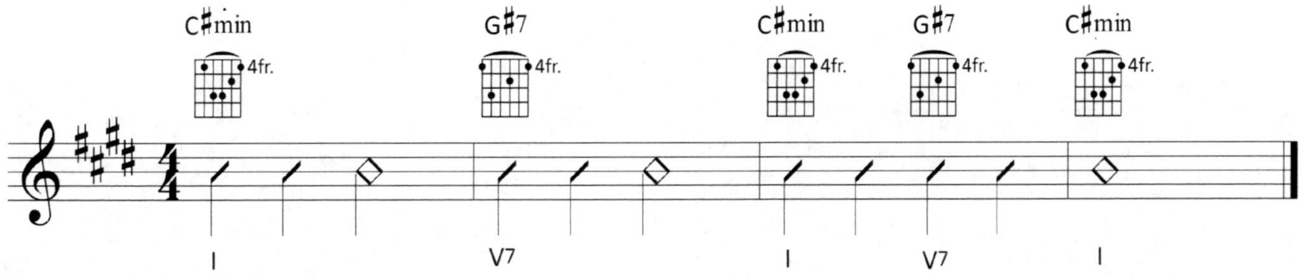

Invention in C# Minor No. 1

AUDIO 44

21
B
25
28
32
B
1.
35
2.
B
rit. . . . .

Invention in C# Minor No. 2

AUDIO 45

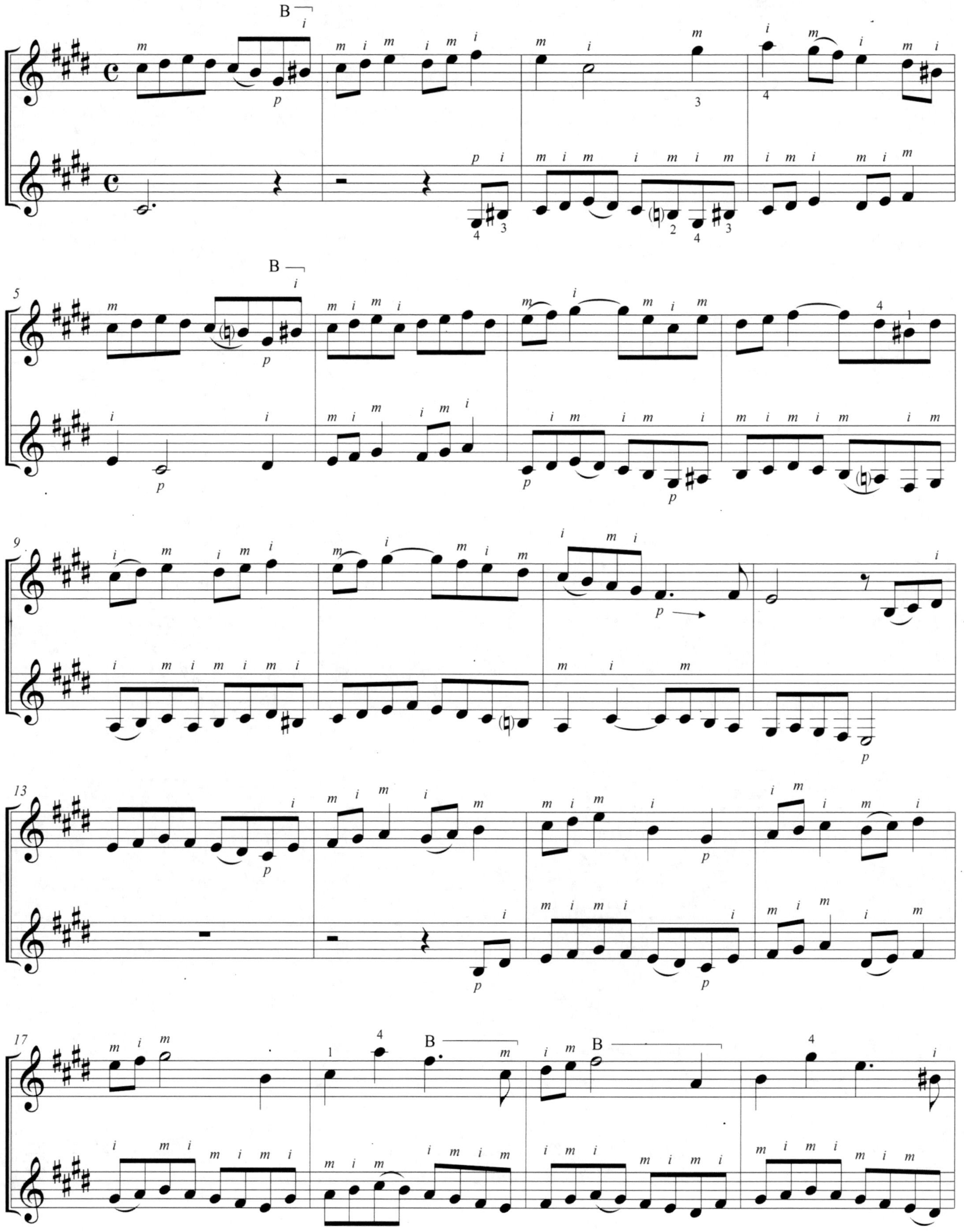

rit. . . . .

Invention in C# Minor No. 3

AUDIO 46

rit. . . . .

RHYTHM DANCE V - PERCUSSIVE TECHNIQUES

Rhythm Dance V (p. 226), in 4/4 includes syncopated dyads in the upper part, while introducing right-hand percussive techniques. The opening right-hand pattern is shown below:

Ex. 38a

The pattern may simply be played exactly as shown above, or with an optional added percussive technique where the fingers and *p* prepare by lightly slapping the strings, producing a subtle clicking sound of fingers on strings.

Ex. 38b

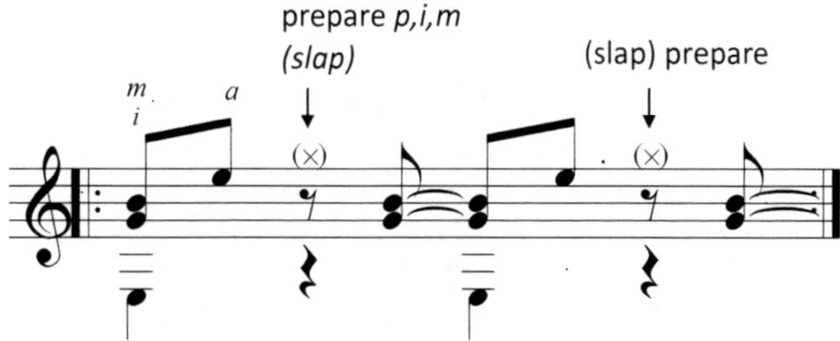

A different kind of percussive technique follows at m. 4 where *p* taps on the soundboard indicated by an × note head:

Ex. 38c

ONE-HAND HARMONIC

Rhythm Dance V also includes a new technique for playing harmonics, involving only the right hand. One-hand harmonics can be played by either *p* or *a*. Proceed as follows:

- Lightly touch (but do not depress) *i* in an extended position on ① directly over fret XII.
- While still touching *i*, stroke ① with either *p* or *a*.
- Immediately release *i*, allowing ① to vibrate freely.

Practice playing one-hand harmonics in the following exercises:

Ex. 39a

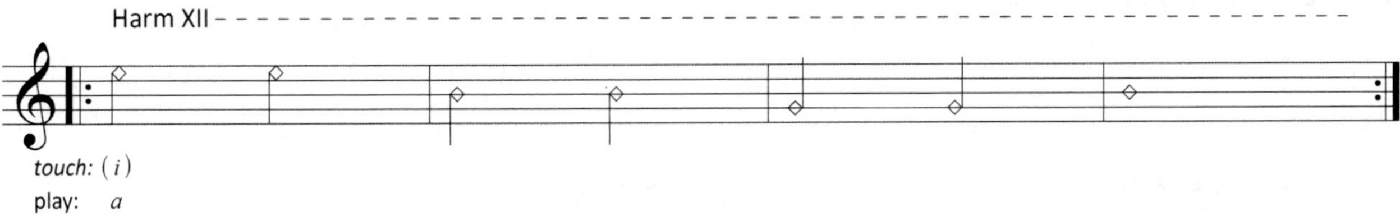

Ex. 39b

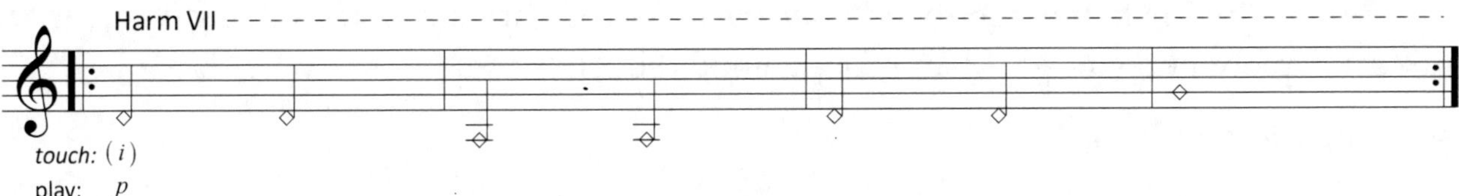

In the final measure of *Rhythm Dance V* is a *one-hand harmonic*. To play, touch *i* at fret XII and simultaneously stroke with *a*.

RHYTHM DANCE VI - MIXED IRREGULAR METER

Rhythm Dance VI (p. 228) also uses the percussive *p* tap but is written in both irregular and mixed meters. It begins with the following $\frac{7}{8}$ pattern, organized as 3 beats, two *simple* and one *compound:*

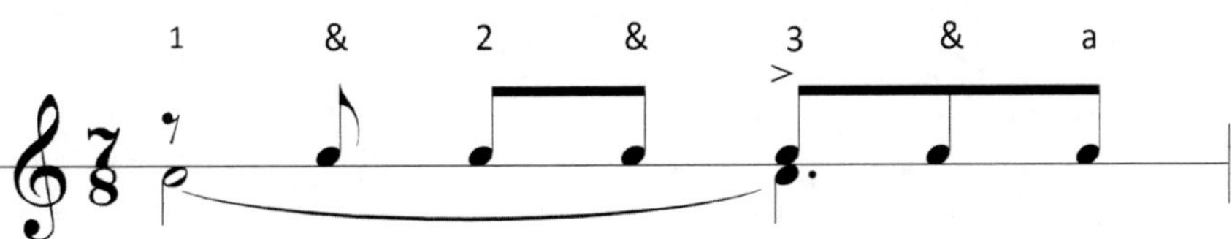

...next, realize the rhythm on open strings and practice counting aloud while playing.

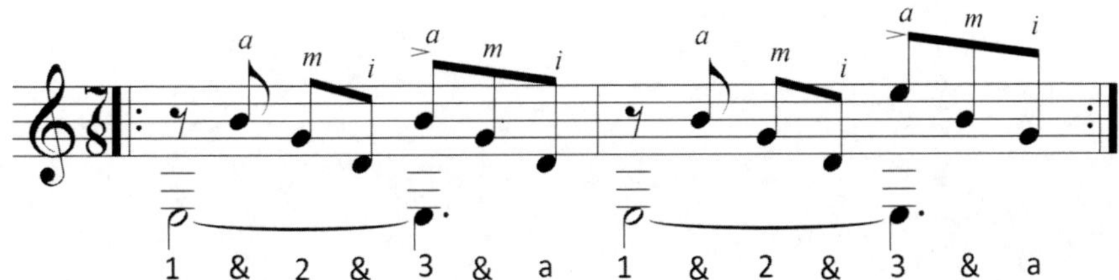

Beginning at m. 17, a mixed, irregular meter is introduced. Practice clapping and counting aloud the following unitl secure. Be sure to stress to the numeric count:

Ex. 40a - count and clap

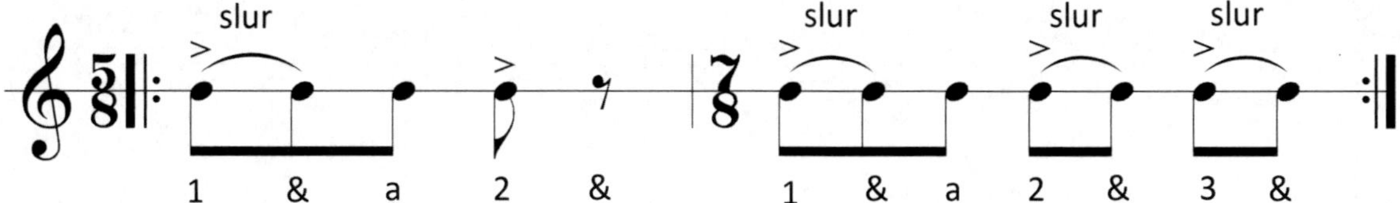

Transfering this rhythm to the right-hand only, the slurred eighth notes pairs change to quarter notes. Next, tap on the soundboard and count aloud the following:

Ex. 40b - tap on soundboard

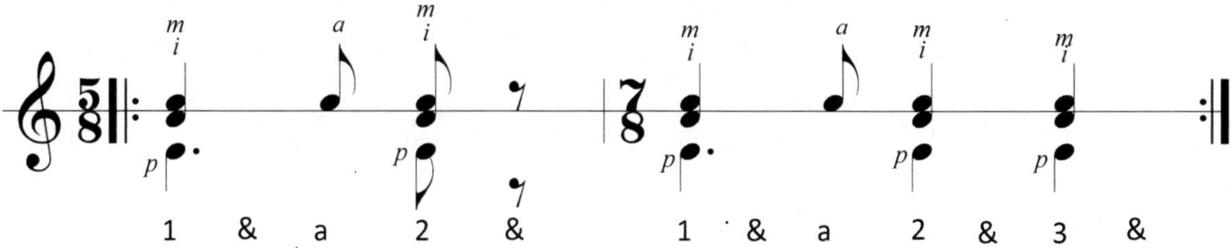

Continue to count aloud and practice the passage on open strings.

Ex. 40c - play and count

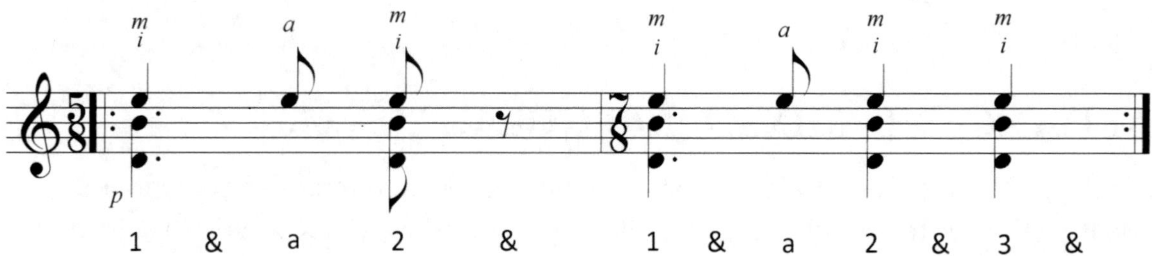

THIS PAGE LEFT INTENTIONALLY BLANK

Rhythm Dance V

cresc
f
gliss
mp
f
B
mf
dim.
rit. . .
a tempo
rit. . .
XII ②
one-handed harm

Rhythm Dance VI

BII⑤
Harm XII

WWW

Repertoire from the Masters

You'll now study works of some of the great composers, drawing from your developed skillset of techniques such as alternating rest and free stroke, barring, slurs, ornaments, harmonics and playing music with counterpoint. In addition, the selections here offer opportunity to apply reading in a variety of keys that you are now familiar with. All the music is from the standard repertoire and has been chronologically organized from the Renaissance to the Romantic period. Consider memorizing any of the selections you find particularly interesting. You'll find a list of other recommended works that are similar in level of difficulty at the online supplement.

Packington's Pound

Francis Cutting (1550-1596)

Fast

mf — *pont.* — *f* — *mp* — *f* — *ord.* — *mf* — *rit. . . . .*

Tarantella

Two Baroque Dances
Gaspar Sanz (1640-1710)
Pavana
Espanoleta
last time rit.

Minuet

from the "Anna Magdalena Notebook"

Christian Petzold (1677-1733)

March

from the "Anna Magdalena Notebook"

C.P.E. Bach (1714-1788)

* F is played 4 at **VI** on ②

** C's are played at **VIII** on ① and ⑥

Sarabande

G. F. Handel (1685-1759)

* Hinge Bar

Barbara Allen

Andante

Op. 35, No. 14

Fernando Sor (1778-1839)

Allegretto Moderato

Op. 31, No. 3

Fernando Sor (1778-1839)

Andantino

Op. 14, No. 10

Mateo Carcassi (1792-1853)

Etude

from the "Schule für die Guitare"

J.K. Mertz (1806-1856)

Tempo di marcia

cresc.

Rondo

from the "Neue Guitarren-Schule"

Fransesco Molino (1775-1847)

* F on ② at **VI**

Two Pieces

Op. 21
Mateo Carcassi (1792-1853)
Andantino
Fine
D.C. al Fine (no repeats)

Valse
Fine
D.C. al Fine (no repeats)

Andantino

Op. 11, No. 4

Mateo Carcassi (1792-1853)

mf
mf
ff

Allegretto
Op. 59, No. 19
M. Carcassi (1792-1853)
mf
f
BIV
p
rit.
(Pos IV)
1.
2.

* B on ① at **VII**